Disney on a Dime

Money-Saving Secrets
for Your Walt Disney World Vacation

Chris & Kristal Carlson

Disney on a Dime

Money-Saving Secrets for Your Walt Disney World Vacation

Published by The Intrepid Traveler

P.O. Box 531

Branford, CT 06405

http://www.intrepidtraveler.com

Copyright ©2006 by Edward Christopher Carlson

First Edition

Printed in the U.S.A.

Cover design by Foster & Foster

Maps by Evora Taylor

Library of Congress Card Number: 2005924120

ISBN-13: 978-1-887140-57-7

ISBN-10: 1-887140-57-3

10 9 8 7 6 5 4 3 2 1

Trademarks, Etc.

This book makes reference to various Disney copyrighted characters, trademarks, marks and registered marks owned by The Walt Disney Company and Disney Enterprises, Inc.

All references to these properties, and to the Twilight Zone®, a registered trademark of CBS, Inc. are made solely for editorial purposes. Neither the authors nor the publisher makes any commercial claim to their use, and neither is affiliated with either The Walt Disney Company or CBS, Inc. in any way.

Dedicated to
our wonderful children,
India, August, Canyon, and Roman,
the Princess and Princes of our home.
Thank you for keeping us young at heart.
May your lives always be filled
with "Disney Magic."

About the Authors

Photo by Joe Klingaman, Creative Fotoworks

Chris and Kristal Carlson are East Texas natives who met in church when they were young, and now reside in northwest Arkansas, where Chris works in merchandising for a major corporation. Chris attended and graduated from the Sam Walton College of Business at the University of Arkansas and received an MBA from Webster University in Fayetteville, Arkansas. Kristal homeschools their four children and is active in the local home schooling community. Chris and Kristal enjoy traveling as a family and are able to do so on a modest salary.

Chris first discovered Disney World in 1988 on a trip with his high school band. He was only there for a few hours but he was hooked. A few years later, he convinced his family to switch their annual vacation to Disney World. "I will never forget the look on my father's face at the ticket window outside Epcot. Our family of eight brought the total bill up to a thousand dollars." When they started bringing their own kids, Chris and Kristal devoted themselves to discovering the secrets of making Walt Disney World affordable for all.

Table of Contents

INTRODUCTION

The Walt Disney World® Resort offers more to do in one location than any other place on earth. If you have never been there, you can believe all the hype about it that you've seen on TV or have heard from friends and family. It's a magical place, one that lives up to its nickname, the "Happiest Place on Earth," for millions of visitors a year.

Less happily, you can easily spend a small fortune taking your family to Disney World. Worse, the hype — and a quick glance at the prices — may give you the impression that you have to spend an arm and a leg to enjoy a Disney World vacation. This is not true!!! Staying at Disney World's top resorts, dining in its most lavish restaurants, and buying all the merchandise it offers, would run you many thousands of dollars in a week's time. But those experiences are simply icing on the cake when it comes to enjoying WDW. You can have a great Disney World vacation without spending a cent on any icing. We know because we've done it, not once but nine times in ten years, with first two and now four children in tow.

In this book we will break down what is vital for your vacation and what is not. We will show you how to save hundreds, if not thousands, of dollars on your Walt Disney World vacation. And we will help you make that vacation a reality by offering specific suggestions for cutting your everyday spending and for making extra money to grow your vacation savings account as quickly as possible.

What "Disney on a Dime" Is NOT:

• A traditional guidebook.

• A book that describes the various parks in detail.

• A book that tells you what rides are best, where to sit, and so on.

• A book that shows you how to ride 40 rides in a day.

• A book that talks about luxury resort options and ways to waste your money.

What "Disney on a Dime" Is:

• A book that offers hundreds of specific tactics and strategies for saving money for and on your Disney World Vacation.

• A book that will help you get the most for every dollar you spend.

You will discover, among other things:

• How to cut your costs in half by being creative and knowing what you can and can't do.

• How the ticket system works and how to use it to your advantage.

• What loopholes exist in the system and how to use them to stretch your budget.

You can reduce your vacation budget by at least $200 by using just one of our tips and by thousands by using all of them. We guarantee it! (See page 223.)

Why We Wrote This Book

We believe that no childhood is complete without a trip to Walt Disney World. So naturally, we wanted our children to have that magical experience while they were still little and thought the characters (Mickey Mouse and friends) were really real and magical. When our two oldest children were small, though, money was tight. We had to find ways to cut expenses in order to go and we succeeded through trial and error. If we had relied on the cost information available online, and from travel agents and Disney, we would have given up before we started.

We wanted to go to Disney World for five days and stay for seven nights. When we looked online we were quoted a price of about $3,500 just for tickets, some food, and lodging — and this was almost a decade ago. We consulted a travel agent and got the same price. Instead of throwing our hands in the air, we looked around for a better deal. We decided to stay offsite, buy tickets on our own (rather than as part of a package), eat the majority of our meals at the hotel, and drive instead of fly. We calculated that if we did that, we could go for around $1,400. We called another travel agent to see if he could beat that. He laughed at us on the phone: "Impossible!" And it was for him, but not for us.

Since that successful experience, we have returned to Disney World many times and have found many more ways to save money and stretch our dollars. By trying out new tricks, keeping our eyes open, and sharing tips with other Disney-loving friends, we have discovered how to go several times a year with four young children and still spend less annually for all our Disney trips than some of our acquaintances spend for a single visit.

Saving money isn't brain surgery; it is easy. You just have to be aware that there are options beyond those you see advertised. You don't have to live in the lap of luxury in order to have a good time. You can have a wonderful time at Disney World on the budget you can afford. In fact, you'll have a better time because you won't be worrying about how long it's going to take you to pay it off.

After watching us take numerous trips to Disney World over the years, friends and acquaintances were constantly asking how we could afford to go so often. Many of them assumed that it had to cost several thousand dollars to make each trip and wondered if we had a secret source of income. A lot of them thought they would never be able to go even once because of the supposed huge expense. We decided we wanted to help people like us make their dream vacation a reality, and *Disney on a Dime* was born.

How This Book Can Help You

Disney on a Dime will help you save money and get more for the money you spend. If you have to watch every penny, you'll find the tips you need to make a Disney World vacation affordable. If you are fortunate enough to have a bigger budget at your disposal, you'll be able to stay longer and do more using the tactics we offer.

We sincerely hope that our book can help families everywhere to make their vacation dreams a reality by stretching those hard earned dollars. Have a magical time!

— *Chris and Kristal Carlson*

Disney on a Dime

What Is Disney World Anyway?

Many people mistake Walt Disney World's original theme park, the Magic Kingdom, for Disney World itself and think that Disney World is the name of a big theme park near Orlando, Florida. But Disney World is so much more. It is a collection of four theme parks, two water parks, numerous resorts, a shopping district, a sports complex, and many golf courses. Its official name is Walt Disney World® Resort but, like most people, we'll refer to it as Disney World, or WDW, for short.

Disney World is truly a magical and immense complex, which is why it costs more than your local amusement park or regional attraction. But while the cost is higher, the value you get in return is hard to match anywhere else. Every Disney World theme park offers first-class entertainment and wonderful rides in a themed environment; they literally take you into a different world and state of mind. You can't see and do everything at WDW in a single day as you can at your local amusement park. You'll need at least four days just to explore its four theme parks, the Magic Kingdom, Epcot, Disney–MGM Studios, and Disney's Animal Kingdom.

The Magic Kingdom was the first and only park at the Walt Disney World Resort from 1971 to 1982, when it was joined by Epcot. The Magic Kingdom, whose icon is Cinderella Castle (the castle you see in all the TV ads) is a must-see for any Disney fan, young or old. Here you'll find classic rides like *Peter Pan's Flight*, *Dumbo the Flying Elephant*, *Pirates of the Caribbean*, and *"it's a small world,"* as well as newer rides based on characters such as Winnie the Pooh, Buzz Lightyear, and Stitch. If you can only go to one park, this is it.

Epcot, the second park, is divided into two areas, Future World and World Showcase. Future World is full of educational and informative rides, plus a few thrill rides, such as *Test Track* and *Mission: SPACE*. World Showcase exposes guests to cultures from around the world. Eleven countries, including the U.S.A., host pavilions (some with movies and rides) that give visitors a glimpse of what it might be like to visit, eat, and live there.

Disney–MGM Studios was added in 1988. It offers shows and productions that give guests a "behind the scenes" look at how movies are made, along with a number of rides, both gentle and thrill. You can ride a roller coaster while rocking out to Aerosmith, see "Beauty and the Beast" on stage, blast off into space in a Star Wars spacecraft, laugh with the Muppets, take a trip through movie history, drop 10 stories in an old elevator, or be amazed as you watch stunt cars leap through the air.

The newest park, Disney's Animal Kingdom, offers live animals and animal-themed exhibits, rides, and shows. The Disney Imagineers (designers) have made the park look like parts of Africa and Asia. If you love nature and animals you will love this park.

With so much to see and do, you can find yourself in a bind at Walt Disney World if you arrive without researching the theme parks, scheduling the time you need to see them, and working out the logistics and finances for your trip. Plan and budget accordingly.

- The Cheapest Time to Go

- Ways to Save for Your Trip

- Ways to Raise Extra Money

- Buy Your Vacation Bit by Bit

- Extra Tips

PLAN!
BUDGET!
SAVE!

Budgeting and saving for a Walt Disney World vacation is different for everyone. For some, it will be a three- or four-year ordeal. For others, it can be a matter of just calling and booking the trip. Whatever the case, it pays to plan and budget carefully, because it is likely to be one of the most expensive trips you ever take.

Will you fly or drive? Stay in a Walt Disney World® Resort hotel ("on-property," as the Disney folks say) or stay offsite? Eat all your meals in restaurants, at fast food counters, or in your room? Visit every single Disney World attraction you can find, or just see one or two theme parks? Stay a day, a week, more, or somewhere in between? And that's just for starters.

A trip to Walt Disney World (WDW) presents a lot of options. Your choices among them will make a big difference in the total cost of your vacation. With a little preparedness, you can prevent wasting a lot of money. Chances are, the better you plan, the more you will be able to save.

Clearly, you need to come up with a game plan, especially if you are going to have to save up the money before you can afford to go on vacation. Taking baby steps is OK. Each step you take will help to keep your vacation from becoming a huge financial blow.

Start with an Estimated Budget and a Time Line

Knowing how much money you'll need and how long it will take you to get it together is your first step to making your Walt Disney World dream a reality. Everything else flows from there. For starters, go to the Disney web site, www.disneyworld.com to get rough estimates of what tickets, hotel, food, travel, and so on will cost you. (Click on the "plan your vacation" icon.) Then use that information to draw up an estimated budget. You can adjust it as you read this book and gather more information.

How much will you need? It depends a good deal on what's important to you. If your major goal is to see the Disney World theme parks with your kids or grandkids, and you are willing to stay in economy lodgings and forego sit-down restaurants, you can keep the costs fairly low. Here is an example of what we have done on some trips in the past. It is a little extreme in that it calls for eating all meals in the hotel room, but it works and keeps the costs low enough to allow most people to go.

Our Budget for 4 days/5 nights
(based on prices as we go to press)

Drive $200
(for gas from Fayetteville, Arkansas)

Hotel & Food En Route $100

Tickets* $710
(base tickets w/ tax for 2 adults and 2 children ages 3 to 9)

Lodging $160
($32 a night offsite)

Meals $ 72
($18 a day for 4 days, all meals eaten in our hotel room)

Snacks & Water $ 30
($7.50 a day for items bought at the grocery store and brought into the parks)

Souvenirs $ 40
($10 per person)

Total   **$1,312**
*See *Chapter Four* for ticket types.

Your transportation costs may differ, but if you figure that you'll have to spend a minimum of $110 to $130 per adult per day once you are in Orlando, you should be in the ballpark. Just remember to add transportation costs and take Disney's seasons into consideration.

The Cheapest Time to Go

Disney has four seasons just like the rest of the world. The only difference is that they aren't labeled winter, spring, summer, and fall. Disney's seasons are Value, Regular, Peak, and Holiday. The seasons are unevenly spread through the year and are determined not by weather or temperature, but by typical consumer vacation habits and attendance at the theme parks.

Value Season is broken into three blocks of time:

- January 1 through mid-February,
- September through the first week in October, and
- Thanksgiving Sunday through mid-December.

Although Disney sometimes offers special rates that make other times of the year equally cost-effective, it is generally cheapest to go during the Value Season.

Attendance is lowest at these times due to school schedules in the fall and winter and colder weather in winter. If you have a flexible schedule, we strongly recommend that you consider going in Value Season because it is the cheapest time to visit. Not only can you book hotels at a lower rate, but also you will find better deals and more of them from Disney and others than at any other time of year.

> *Tip:* You will also be able to see and do more in less time because, with fewer people in the parks, you will spend less time in line.

Regular Season is broken up into two blocks of time:

- Mid-April through August, and
- October through Thanksgiving Saturday

Surprisingly perhaps, the summer months are considered a moderate time of the year for Disney World. Rooms at the WDW hotels may be discounted a little, but typically, you won't find any deep discounts there or at other area hotels. If traffic slows, however, they will kick in with some last-minute deals to attract more visitors.

If you plan on going during the summer months (the only time a lot of people can go), do take the heat into consideration. In February and March, Orlando's heat and humidity can get anyone flustered and overheated. In June, July, and August, it can be a little too much to handle. If you go then, take precautions to ensure that everyone stays hydrated and is protected from the sun.

The crowds will vary from day to day and from park to park at this time of year, but expect crowds and lines to be heavy on most days. If you don't like crowds, avoid the Fourth of July, Halloween, and Thanksgiving weekend. July Fourth is supposedly one of the busiest days of the year at WDW. The parking lot entrance gates are usually closed before noon due to capacity limits — which means the parks are essentially closed to later arrivals, except Disney's resort hotel guests who come via WDW transport. Halloween is celebrated for much of October, and Thanksgiving weekend is packed.

Peak Season is centered around Spring Break and occupies just one block of time:

> • Mid-February through mid-April.

This time of year is considered the most crowded, but we find it hit or miss. Some days you need to hold onto your kids for dear life in order to stay together. Other times there is hardly anyone around. But you can be assured that at some point during your vacation you will encounter a lot of people if you visit at Peak Season. President's Day week, Mardi Gras, and Easter will almost certainly be crowded. However, the week after President's Day week tends to be very light as do weeks in early April. Most schools have Spring Break in March.

> *Note:* As always, there are trade-offs. When the crowds are larger, the theme parks tend to stay open longer and offer more shows, special events, and rides. In fact, some older rides are only open seasonally, because it doesn't make economic sense to keep all the rides open when attendance is low. Bear in mind that "low" is a relative term. A slow day for Disney is likely to seem pretty jam-packed to many visitors, especially in the Magic Kingdom.

Holiday Season is Christmastime:

> • Mid-December through December 31.

This can be a very tough time to get a room in the Orlando area. Many families have made Christmas morning in the WDW theme parks an annual tradition. The hotels fill up fast in and out of WDW. It will be crowded and, most likely, moderately cold. In fact, it may be very cold. Orlando's temperature can drop into the twenties, although it seldom does so and rarely in December.

Tip: Disney puts on quite a show for the holidays, with special decorations, shows, and activities that will keep you in the holiday spirit from morning until late at night. If you'd like to participate but can't afford to pay top dollar, try to take your vacation in the first two weeks of December, during the post-Thanksgiving Value Season. The Christmas festivities will be in full swing but the crowds and the prices will be among the lowest of the year.

Start your planning with a free DVD

You can order a free vacation planning kit that includes a planning DVD at www.disneyworld.com. The DVD includes over an hour of commentary about the WDW theme parks along with an in-depth look at the different WDW resorts to give you a better understanding of what Disney World is all about. It comes with a CD-ROM that lets you move interactively through the many stages of your vacation to help you plan.

Note: This is also a great tool for getting children excited about the trip. Children will watch it over and over. Anticipation builds with each viewing, strengthening the kids' motivation to save their pennies for the big trip ahead.

What you won't find in the DVD and CD are great money-saving tips. That's where we come in.

Ways to Save for Your Trip

This book goes into great detail about ways to cut the overall cost of a Disney World vacation. But even if you use every one of them, you will still need to have a decent amount of money set aside for your trip.

Here are some suggestions for getting the funds together that have worked for us over the years:

Make It a Family Project

Planning and saving for a Disney World trip brings the family together. Make it a project and get the kids to pitch in. Have regular family meetings to chart your progress. Who doesn't want to go to Walt Disney World? Cut everyday costs and put the savings into a vacation fund.

Cost Cutting and Saving Work Hand in Hand

• **Use the classic coin jar.** Months in advance of your trip, set aside a large jar or other container to collect coins. At the end of each day, have every member of the family contribute the loose change from their pockets. Do not give into temptation and raid the jar.

Periodically, roll up the coins and deposit them into your vacation account (see below).

> *Note:* Bank policies on accepting coins vary. Some banks have machines that will count up the loose change for you and exchange it for bills. Others will require you to roll up the coins yourself using coin wrappers. Still others will refuse your coins altogether or will exchange them for bills only if you have an account with them. Search around for a bank that will cooperate.

> *Caution:* Many grocery stores have Coinstar machines that will count your coins for you and then give you a receipt, which you take to a cashier to get your bills. It's convenient, but you have to pay an 8% to 10% service charge.

• **Another tip for the coin jar**. Instead of casually emptying your pockets or cleaning under the couch cushions or car seats for change, go after it aggressively. Make it a family policy to not buy anything with coins. If something costs $1.05, for example, pay with two $1.00 bills and deposit the 95 cents change into your coin jar. Do this religiously and your savings will grow at a faster pace. The money you're saving won't be missed!

• **Open a vacation savings account at your bank.** Deposit your coin-jar money here, along with any rebate checks, income tax refunds, or money you raise. Having a special account for your vacation savings will not only help you save, but will also help to keep you honest when you spend. Get a check/debit card with your account so that you can conveniently pay for vacation items directly from your vacation savings. This will come in handy when booking hotels, rental cars, and plane tickets before your trip, and you will be able to draw on it during your vacation wherever credit cards are accepted — which means you will be less tempted to dip into other accounts or charge vacation expenses to your credit card and build up a big debt.

> *Note:* We live in Arkansas, where local banks offer free "Vacation Accounts." If you can't open a free account locally, shop online for a bank that will let you do so. For example, www.ing.com offers a free account that pays interest on your deposits.

It pays to shop around. A few years ago, an online bank was paying depositors $25.00 for each new account they opened. We set up a savings account for each member of the family — Mom, Dad, and four kids — giving us an extra $150.00 right off the bat.

• **Break a habit and put the savings into your coin jar** or vacation account. Let's look at the most obvious candidates:

Stop smoking (or at least cut back). Cigarettes cost a fortune. Most people can save $5 to $10 a day by quitting.

Kick the morning goodie habit. Do you stop off at Starbucks or the local donut or coffee shop every morning? Is this really a wise investment of $5 or more a day? Stop making your daily stop, and put the money you would have spent on lattes and sugary sweets into your savings jar. You'll be surprised at how fast this adds up.

Take your lunch to work. Eating your midday meal out every day will run you $8 to $15 a day at almost any sit-down restaurant. Make the sacrifice: brown-bag it and take your family to Disney World instead.

$$aver Tip: If you have to go out for lunch, try to cut something out. Order water with your meal instead of coffee or a soft drink. Don't order a dessert or any extras. In fact, have an appetizer or side salad as a meal. It will be cheaper — and think of the calories you may save.

Limit your soda and snack consumption. If you are an avid soda drinker, save by buying two-liter bottles or generic-brand canned sodas and bringing them into work instead of purchasing drinks from the soda machine or snack shop. If you think doing this might embarrass you, try it. You'll be surprised at how many people think it's a great idea.

The key here, of course, is to make sure the money you save actually gets saved and not merely spent on something else.

• **Use coupons when you grocery shop** and put aside the money you save from your grocery budget each week. Again, the key is to keep track and make sure you put the saved money aside for your trip.

• **Save a specific amount from every paycheck**. If your employer gives you the option, have a certain amount automatically deposited into your vacation savings account, so that you're not tempted to spend it on anything else. Even $10 or $20 a pay period adds up to serious money over time.

• **Borrow from the library instead of buying or renting.** Instead of renting videos and DVDs, borrow them from the library. Instead of buying books, borrow them. Some libraries even loan artwork. Take full advantage of what you can get for free whenever you can. Just remember to return items on time so that you don't run up any fines.

Cut Your Monthly Bills

• **Shrink your cable package** by cutting your movie channels and extended packages.

• **Cut your phone costs** by dropping your cell phone service or by eliminating your home phone and using a cell phone as your primary line.

• **Bundle telecommunications services** to qualify for discounts. Seek out providers that will give you a discount if you combine Internet and cable services, or Internet, long distance, and local phone services.

Ways to Raise Extra Money

Cutting costs and applying the savings toward your vacation may not give you enough to pay for your Disney World trip. You may also have to raise money. Here are some things you can do to fatten your vacation budget:

Sell What You're Not Using

Go through your house and get rid of all your old stuff. Do some spring (or summer, fall, or winter) cleaning and assess what you can live without. Get ruthless, and sell anything you aren't using.

• **Have garage sales or yard sales**. You'd be amazed at how much you can raise from a garage sale. Old clothes, toys, and gadgets you never use can bring in cash that really adds up.

> *Tip:* Ask around to see if your friends or family have things they might want to "donate" to your cause.

• **Sell large items through newspaper ads**. Do you have an extra bedroom set, TV, car, or couch? Don't try to sell bigger ticket items at a garage sale. People show up at garage sales with a limited amount of money and they are typically looking for smaller things. Instead, advertise them in the local newspaper.

> *$$aver Tip:* Some newspapers will allow you to list certain items

for free. Call and check out their policies.

• **Sell your stuff on eBay (www.ebay.com)**. If you have name brand items or collectibles like baseball cards, figurines, vases, and so on that have a higher-than-garage-sale value, consider selling them on eBay. Items that have no value to most people can fetch high dollars on eBay.

> *Tip:* If you do not have an account with eBay, get one. It is a great resource for finding deals and selling items. Setting up an account is extremely easy. You pay nothing to join and minimal fees (25¢ to a maximum of $4.80 as of this writing) to list items for sale. eBay gets 1.50% to 5.25% of the final selling price. So if you sold an item for $10, you'd pay eBay a total of 78 cents.

• **Sell used books on Half.com or Amazon.com**. Half.com is owned by eBay and focuses on books and media items. You pay nothing to join or list items, unlike on eBay, but the fee structure is different. Half.com collects a bit more — from 15% (for items selling for under $50) to 5% (for items selling for over $500) of the selling price. So if you sold a book for $10, Half.com would collect $1.50.

Amazon.com is a great place to sell books with no upfront fees. It allows you to list as many items as you want and doesn't charge you for posting them. (Some people put up several hundred books.) You do not have to work out payment arrangements with buyers, as you do when using eBay, because Amazon collects the money from the buyer and deposits it into your bank account after taking out its fee. The trade-off is that you pay Amazon a bit more than you'd pay Half.com.

Take a Part-Time or Temporary Job

• **Check out temporary jobs**. Around the holidays, for example, many stores or vendors in malls look for temporary help just for the Holiday Season. These jobs typically have very flexible hours and last for a short time. Just be sure you stash the money in your vacation account and don't spend it on gifts.

• **Take on a paper route**. Paper routes are not just for kids anymore. Take on a paper route for six months or so. Getting up early every morning for six months could wear on you a little, but if a route paid $500 a month, you could save up $3,000 for your vacation very quickly. In our area, you'd typically spend two to four hours each morning delivering papers and earn a bit more, $600 to $700 a month.

Enlist the Kids

Kids can be very enterprising when they feel motivated. Encourage them to build up some vacation savings of their own. Kids in kindergarten and primary grades could open a lemonade stand or collect and redeem empty cans and bottles. Middle-schoolers could offer their services for weed-pulling, window washing, or running errands. Their older siblings might build a nice nest egg mowing lawns, washing windows, babysitting, walking dogs, or caring for houseplants while their owners are away. Encourage them. Kids are natural entrepreneurs.

Buy Your Vacation Bit by Bit

It used to seem that right before we took a big (or small) trip, we suddenly had to make a huge, unexpected visit to the store for extra snacks, flip-flops, sunglasses, coolers, soft drinks, and other vacation essentials. Such spending can put your vacation budget into a hole before you start, especially if you end up having to buy the items at a destination like Disney World, where they charge a premium. Eventually, we learned to plan and buy ahead so that we didn't break the bank just before our vacation. Better yet, we actually save money now by anticipating our needs and buying most of the essentials when they are on sale.

> *Note:* This strategy saves headaches as well as money because it gives you plenty of time to find what you need.

Buy as You Go: It's Easier than You Think

Planning a Disney trip can take a year or two. Take advantage of the opportunities to save that can come along during that time. Think of your trip whenever you see a sale. When you go grocery shopping, for example, think about the non-perishables you can buy ahead and pick them up when they are on special. Buy summer clearance items during the fall in preparation for your trip in the spring or the following summer.

> *Note:* Items like bathing suits and sunscreen may not be easily available in your local stores year-round, and they will cost a fortune if you wait to buy them at Disney World. A friend of ours, for example, spent $13 for a small bottle of sunblock at a Disney Resort gift shop. Plan to pack whatever you might possibly need on your vacation and bring it with you.

• **Anticipate your vacation needs**. It is important to think through your vacation and consider what you will need in the way of clothing, toiletries, cosmetics, snacks, toys, and so on. *Chapter Ten: What to Pack*, offers extensive checklists to help you remember everything, along with special tips on what to buy well in advance of your vacation. Remember, even having to buy basic toiletry items that you forgot at home can take a chunk out of your vacation spending money.

Also consider the different types of clothing you may need. Florida weather can be unpredictable. If you pack only shorts and t-shirts for a spring trip, you may have to shell out money for new clothes if the temperature drops down to 50 degrees when an unexpected cold front blows through. The same goes for not packing for hot weather in the winter. Raincoats or ponchos are a must any time of the year and can be costly if purchased inside the theme parks. Ponchos, for example, run about $6 each in the parks — which adds up to $24 for a family of four. Planning can and will save you money.

• **Bring the "souvenirs" with you**. Buying "souvenirs" before your trip (see *Chapter Five*) may seem odd, but many of the entertainment items sold in the Disney World theme parks are available elsewhere, for a lot less. Buy ahead and you won't have to pay for them on Disney's terms. For example, when it gets dark in the parks, vendors come out of the woodwork with carts full of outrageously priced glow-in-the-dark wands, bracelets, and other items that make the nighttime fun. The kids just love this stuff and find them equally appealing with or without the Disney logo. (Who can see a logo in the dark?) Plan ahead and buy such "souvenirs" before you go. You'll find plenty of them at such sites as: www.orientaltrading.com and www.eBay.com. Or try shopping for them at dollar stores and other discount outlets.

Spread Out Payments for Tickets and Lodging

Here, too, you don't have to pay for everything at once. With a bit of planning, you can arrange to buy things a little at a time.

• **Buy theme park admission tickets before you go.** Tickets are one of the biggest expenses of a Walt Disney World vacation (see *Chapter Four* for prices and options). Buy one every couple of months as your vacation funds grow, and you'll leave for vacation with a large part of your expenses already paid for. Park tickets are good until used, and Annual Passes do not expire until one year from the day they are activated (not purchased). You can buy tickets online at www.disneyworld.com, through travel agents, and at the Disney Stores

— except for Annual Passes, which can only be purchased from Disney online or at the parks.

• **Book your rooms through Disney if you plan to stay at WDW.** If you plan to book your vacation through Disney and stay onsite, then do it now and pay it off over time. You may pay a bit more, but you'll have the advantage of interest-free financing for up to two years. Disney will require a percentage of the package up front. The rest can be paid over time as long as it is paid off 45 days before your arrival date. (See "Extra Tips," *Chapter Six* for additional details and tips.)

• **Shop ahead for flights**. If you plan to fly to Disney World, acquaint yourself with the discount airlines that fly from your local airport(s), and keep your eyes open for airline sales. You can generally book air tickets up to a year in advance. So if you plan to fly, shop around for the best deals as soon as you have approximate dates for your trip. Once you know how much the flights may cost, make sure you have a plan to save the money. When you have it, buy all your tickets at once so that you are assured that everyone in your group will be on the same flight. Your flights will be paid off far in advance of your trip.

> *Caution:* Unless you are absolutely positive about your travel dates, do not buy non-refundable tickets even though they are the cheapest. They can be a waste of money if you have to change them, because the change fees will cost you more than what you saved by buying them.

• **Get your car in shape if you plan to drive.** Be sure your car is road worthy long before you go. Schedule needed maintenance and repairs weeks before your departure to avoid nasty surprises and ensure that the cost won't eat into your vacation budget.

Extra Tips for Planning and Saving from "Disney on a Dime"

Make planning and saving a family activity. Get everyone involved in vacation planning. Let the kids know the costs that are involved and how if everyone works together, a Disney World vacation could become a reality. Then set goals and expectations with your family. Have weekly or monthly meetings to count your vacation funds, look at how close you are to your goals, and set new goals for the upcoming time period. With everyone working together, the funds are likely to grow more quickly than if Mom and Dad try to go it alone without the kids' help.

Cut yourself some financial slack during your vacation by adding an extra 10%, say, to your monthly utility-bill payments. Then, when you take your vacation, you won't have to pay utility bills that month because you'll have a credit with the utility companies. Many utility companies allow this.

Use layaway to buy items for your trip. Say you are planning to camp at Disney World and that special tent that you've had your eye on goes on sale. If you don't yet have the funds on hand, grab it and leverage the free financing that layaway offers. Most major retailers offer such plans. They let you purchase items by making a down payment and paying the balance over a period of time.

Wal-Mart offers one of the most popular and widely used layaway plans. It lets you layaway an item by putting 10% down and paying the balance in 60 days. If you aren't able to complete the transaction in 60 days, or if you change your mind, you simply get back the money that you put down.

Annualize your costs and savings. When calculating the potential savings that can be made by stopping or starting an activity, think of the savings in yearly instead of daily terms. For example, if you decide to stop your daily trip to Starbucks in order to help fund your Disney vacation, do not think of the savings as a mere $5 a day, think of it as $25 a week or $1,300 a year. Thinking of the $1,300 you're saving by sacrificing your morning treat will do a lot more to keep you on the straight and narrow if you're tempted to indulge yourself "just this once," than thinking of just $5 a day.

Apply this same way of thinking to your vacation spending. You might think that $50 is not too bad a price for a nice dinner for you and your family. But if you are going to stay at Disney for a week, think of the cost of dinners for your whole trip. Seven dinners at $50 each adds up to $350 for the week, and you'll still have breakfast, lunch, and snacks to pay for. Costs can add up quickly if you don't look at the whole picture.

Budget more than you think you'll need. You can save a lot of money by using the advice in this book, but unexpected events can and will happen. So while you are planning, also plan for things not to go as planned. Budget for that flat tire, extra night at the hotel, plane layover, or whatever else can befall someone on vacation, and have some emergency money saved just in case.

Check Disney and weather web sites immediately before your trip. Get the latest information on park hours, what rides and attractions are open, and what special activities will be going on during your visit. Also check the weather forecast for the Orlando area and then double-check your packing list to be sure you're prepared for it. Disney-related sites to check include:

> www.allearsnet.com
> www.wdwmagic.com
> www.mousesavers.com
> www.pocketdisney.com (let's you download schedules onto a PDA or cell phone)

You'll find the Orlando forecast at almost any weather site, including:

> www.weather.com

Don't put all your vacation eggs in the WDW Basket. Taking a trip to Walt Disney World every year is out of the question for most people. For some, it will be the most expensive trip of their lifetimes — even using all the money-saving tips you'll find in the chapters that follow. But that doesn't mean you should go without a vacation for a year or more while you're saving for Disney. Everyone needs a break, and a year seems a lot longer to a child than it does to an adult. So instead, try to alternate low-cost and higher-cost vacations every year or two. If you won't have enough money to go to WDW this year or the next, take a couple of smaller trips, or stay local, while you save for the big one to come.

- Driving Could Be Cheaper

- When Flying Makes Sense

- A Fly / Drive Cost Comparison

- Taking a Bus

- Extra Tips

SAVE ON TRAVEL

One of the downsides to vacationing at Walt Disney World is its location in Orlando, Florida. Orlando is perfect in terms of year-round climate and the nearby beaches, but it is out of the way for almost everybody. Getting to central Florida is a chore, and once there, getting to Walt Disney World can be another journey in and of itself. How you choose to travel can have a huge effect on your vacation budget. Should you drive? Should you fly? Should you carpool, rent a car, or take a bus? How do you find the best deals? And what should you expect to pay?

For some the only option is to fly; for others, to drive. But for many, the decision is not so clear cut. Let's look at the alternatives and issues you will need to address to save sensibly on your travel.

Driving Could Be Cheaper

Unless you can find a deeply discounted airplane ticket, driving may be the most economical means of transportation. Ticket fares can add up quickly for a small to large family. From most places the standard rate for a ticket could be around $300. A family of four would spend $1200 on tickets, which is money that they could be spending on other parts of the vacation.

Here are some tools you can use to help you evaluate your situation and how much you should budget. There are computer programs that cost around $15-$20 that will map out your trip. A popular program is Microsoft's *Streets and Trips*. By putting in your starting point and destination (Lake Buena Vista, Florida, home to Walt Disney World), the program will lay out your trip for you. It will tell you how many miles you will be driving, how long the trip will be, how much gas you will use, and how much it will cost. You can modify the program by changing the driving speeds, how much gas your vehicle uses, how much gas actually costs, and how often you would want to stop and rest.

A cheaper way could be go to www.mapquest.com or www.maps.yahoo.com and use their maps for free. It will tell you the miles and rough time that it takes to get there. From our experience, the time that is stated on the site is slightly more than it really takes. The site will not allow you to adjust speeds or take alternate routes. Also, you will not be able to schedule breaks, adjust miles per gallon, or even see how much the trip will cost. It is a helpful tool that can at least give you a ballpark figure of how many miles and the time that it could take. You could figure out the miles per gallon and price per gallon yourself in order to come up with the costs that would be involved to purchase the gas.

When figuring the gas that is involved with driving, you may want to consult www.fuelcostcalculator.com and www.gasbuddy.com to get an idea of how much to budget. Also remember to include, or at least budget for, extra expenses that could include better tires, oil change, other fluid changes, and/or repairs that must be done to prepare your vehicle for the long trip. It would be a shame to waste time and souvenir or food money on last-minute car repairs. For the most part, these things should be done anyway and shouldn't be part of your trip budget, but if you don't budget for them, they could eat into your slush fund.

Renting a Car

Most people figure that if they're driving, they'll drive their own car. This may not be the most economical way to go. After you consider your car's overall condition, gas mileage, and the wear and tear the long trip will put on your car, you may find that renting a car makes more sense. Let's look at these issues:

• **Does your vehicle need maintenance?** If your car will need new belts, tires, and other repairs to make it road worthy for a long trip, you may be better off renting a car. If your car breaks down in the middle of nowhere, it could cost more than your whole vacation budget to fix it. With a rental car, the rental company will cover most mishaps.

• **Do you want the extra wear and tear on your car?** Putting an extra 3,000 to 5,000 miles on your vehicle not only wears down your vehicle, but also can drive down the overall value of you car. Don't tear up your vehicle to go on vacation. Tear up somebody else's vehicle instead.

• **How is your gas mileage?** A rental might let you economize on fuel, especially if you could rent a smaller car than you currently drive. Consider the savings that can come from using a smaller vehicle. For example, if your vehicle seats seven, but you only need seating for four on your trip, renting a car could be a good option. The difference in cost between fueling a Chevy Suburban and a Ford Focus, for example, is significant, with the car getting about 30 mpg to the SUV's 15 mpg.

• **Consider renting a bigger vehicle and sharing it with friends**. A minivan or SUV can hold up to eight people. Bigger vans can hold 12 to 15. If friends or relatives are going to Disney World at the same time you are, you might all save money by sharing a large rental vehicle. Calculate the possible fuel savings with a bigger vehicle. Not only could you save money, but it could also make the trip more enjoyable if everyone rides together. Just be sure to take into account scheduling issues among family or friends when at WDW.

If you decide to rent

• **Look for weekly rates.** Weekly rates are better than daily rates. So always ask for the weekly rate. If possible try to rent for eight days as there are extra savings in renting for more than a week.

• **Get a vehicle with unlimited miles.** Do not rent a vehicle from a company that tacks on extra charges for each mile you drive. Such charges can more than double the cost of a car rental. The only way a rental that includes mileage charges could work for you is if the car comes with enough free miles to get you to and around Disney World and back home again — a fairly unlikely scenario. Most car rentals today offer unlimited free miles. Make sure you are clear on this before signing the rental agreement. Be careful: some companies offer unlimited miles, but only if the car remains in the state or within a certain area.

• **Price all sizes when looking for a vehicle.** You not only want to know all the options, but also the rental companies may be out of the size vehicle you think you want (a standard compact or mid-sized car, for example) and be willing to upgrade you to a larger size or more luxurious model at no extra cost rather than have you walk away. It never hurts to ask for a free upgrade when picking up your vehicle.

• **Consider upgrading to a minivan with a built-in car seat** if you will need to rent an extra car seat for your trip. Some rental companies charge extra for car-seat rentals. When that's the case, look at the difference in cost between the extra charge and an upgrade to a minivan with a built-in car seat. If the upgrade charge is modest, you could get a bigger vehicle and a car seat for just a little bit more than the additional amount you'd have to pay for the car seat.

> *Note:* In both cases above, be sure to consider engine size and gas mileage. It might be nice to have a larger vehicle, but it could cost you more than it's worth at the pump.

• **Check out web sites for rental discounts.** Look at www.disneyonadime. com for the latest discounts and links to discount sites. Look at our web site and the companies' web sites to ensure that you are getting the best deal.

• **Don't hesitate to cancel reservations if new, lower rates are published.** Just rebook. Keep checking the rental car's web site, along with other rental company sites to find the best deal. If a better deal, special, or upgrade comes out, cancel your previous reservation, and make a new one. Most car rental companies do not charge a penalty for cancellations as long as you cancel within the required amount of time.

> *Caution:* Just be sure the special is available *before* you cancel your reservation.

The following are some rental car web sites you may want to consult:

> www.enterprise.com
> www.budget.com
> www.dollar.com
> www.hertz.com
> www.thrifty.com

Or try these smaller companies:

> Continental Rent-a-Car: www.continentalcar.com, 1-800-656-4223
> Fox Rent-a-Car: www.foxrentacar.com, 1-800-225-4369
> EZ Rent-a-Car: www.e-zrentacar.com, 1-407-850-0607

Eating and Sleeping En Route

There's an old saying that an army moves on its stomach. Families move that way, too. So you'll need to plan and budget for snacks, drinks, and meals on the road if you decide to drive to Disney World. One of the best ways to save is to pack some or all of the food and beverages you'll consume on the way. This is the classic way to travel that many people have forgotten about in recent years.

Calculate the number of meals, snacks, and drinks you will need on the road. Then get out the cooler and pack it accordingly. The cost of buying food and drinks on the road can add up quickly, especially for a large family. Convenience stores aren't known for their cheap drinks and snacks. Typically, they charge more for a 20-ounce soda than you would pay for a two-liter bottle at a grocery store.

If you don't want to make sandwiches and such on the road, pre-make them and store them in Tupperware or similar containers. With a little bit of preparation, you can easily avoid wasting money on the road.

> *Note:* There's an added advantage to packing your meals if your kids are picky eaters: you know you will be able to feed them food they like. That's likely to make the drive considerably happier for everyone.

Finding cheap but decent hotels en route is your other challenge if you'll be on the road long enough to require an overnight stay. Here are some tactics that have worked for us over the years:

• **Book a hotel online if you know where you'll stop.** If your drive is long enough that it requires a stopover on the way to and from Disney World, you may be able to save by booking ahead online. Use the tips in *Chapter Eight* to get the best price and location. Remember, it is sometimes better to have the peace of mind of knowing you have a place to lay your head than to try to save a couple of bucks by waiting until you are on the road to try to find one.

• **Save with coupon/travel books.** Hotels advertise in many coupon/travel books that you can pick up free at convenience stores, gas stations, and rest stops along your route. When you enter a new state, look for a new coupon book. In the past, we have been able to stay at nice three- and four-star hotels for $30 a night using these books. The catch with the coupon books is that most of the coupons are good for only one night and you cannot reserve a room in advance. Also, be sure to read the fine print; a lot of coupons are void on weekends and during holidays.

• **Use your cell phone to call hotels from the road.** If you use a coupon book, start calling ahead to make sure there is availability and to clear up any doubts about the facilities. If you aren't sure where you might stop for the night, draw up a list of possibilities along your route and then call places where you'd like to stay when your stopping point becomes clear. Calling ahead will not only save you the headache (and cost) of driving from one place to another looking for a room but will also let you ask for additional directions if the directions you have aren't very clear.

> *$$aver Tip:* Call more than one hotel in the area. See if any of them will honor a better coupon from another hotel. Doing this could win you upgrades like an indoor pool, a free continental

breakfast, or a location more convenient to the highway. Remember, it never hurts to ask.

• **Look for the "Free Breakfast."** It is always worth it to get that free meal before hitting the road again. Before checking in, ask what is included in the breakfast. The term "continental breakfast" has taken on several different meanings over the years. The meal could be as simple as a package of powdered donuts and a carton of milk or as lavish as waffles, toast, cereal, juice, and the works.

> *Note:* A lot of nicer hotels have onsite restaurants, which do not offer a free breakfast. Be sure to consider that when figuring which hotel offers the best deal. A $30 stay that does not include breakfast (which could cost you $20 to $30 if you haven't packed food) is a bad deal compared to a $35 to $40 stay that does.

When Flying Makes Sense

Flying may actually be cheaper, as well as easier on you. Take into account the time you'll save by flying instead of driving. If you only have a week of vacation, you may not want to spend two to four days driving. A two- to three-hour flight might be a better option. It is important to figure in the value of your time. If flying is the option you prefer — or a must simply because of your vacation schedule and the drive time involved — you may need to give yourself extra time to save for your WDW vacation. Push back your trip by a few months if you need to and save for the extra expense.

Find the Lowest Practical Fare

• **Get to know your local airport(s).** What airlines fly there? If your airport is served by a discount carrier such as Song or Spirit, there's a pretty good chance it will offer low-cost flights to Orlando. Ditto if you live near a busy metropolitan area airport that is served by many different carriers. You may be able to find "fun fares" as low as $35 one-way to Orlando.

• **Fly when traffic is slower.** Orlando is one of the world's top tourist destinations, but the volume of visitors varies seasonally (see *Chapter One*). It can also be affected by weather and world events. When there is a lull in guests going to Disney World, you can be guaranteed that the fares will drop. Take advantage of these patterns if you can.

• **Use all of the free web sites available.** There are numerous web sites and online services available that can help you find the best rate on your flight.

Look around and see who has the best offer. These sites are free and can help you determine what to expect in terms of the cost per person. Most airline ticket sites just have a quoted price, but Priceline allows you to name your own price. Be warned that by naming your own price, you will not be able to choose your airline or the times that the flights will be. Hotwire is a good site, but it also will not allow you to choose the times or carriers.

> www.priceline.com
> www.expedia.com
> www.travelocity.com
> www.cheaptickets.com
> www.orbitz.com
> www.hotwired.com
> www.itasoftware.com (You can't book flights on this site, but you can search fares from your local airport plus alternative airports up to 300 miles away. You determine the number of miles.)
> www.southwest.com
> www.aa.com
> www.united.com
> www.delta.com

• **Get on travel agents' email and call lists for special deals.** Many travel agents keep a list of clients who are flexible about travel dates or who are looking for special deals. They will call or email if something special comes up that you are looking for. Other travel agents keep a fax or email list and they will email out lists of special deals and offers on a weekly basis. To find them, ask friends, check the ads in the Sunday newspaper travel section, and look in the phone book. Then call the agents and ask to be put on their list if they have one.

Remember, travel agents do not require an exclusive contract in order to do business with you. Sign up with as many agents as you can. They work for you and not the other way around. To find them, ask friends about agents they've worked with and consult the phone book and Internet. Then call the agents to see if they will email you about deals for Disney World.

• **Sign up with online travel groups that track the latest deals**. Many travel sites, such as the popular www.travelzoo.com, send out a weekly list of specials and deals. All you have to do is give them your email address, and they do the rest. At least half of the time these lists will contain some savings dealing with Orlando.

When signing up for these services it might be best to use a temporary or "junk" email account. This way your inbox won't be stuffed and you won't have to worry either about having to unsubscribe to all of the groups after your vacation or about them sharing your email with other companies.

• **Plan to fly mid-week or on Saturday.** Be flexible with travel dates. It's often cheaper to fly mid-week than on Friday. Try different days and times. Experts say Tuesday, Wednesday, and Saturday are some of the cheaper days to fly.

When looking at flights, also try to look at different times of the year. Slow travel times can have built-in discounts or can trigger discounts. Play around with the free web sites that allow you to check on the latest flights.

• **Consider alternate airports** near your home and in the Orlando area. Looking for alternate airports could produce some significant savings. This strategy is especially viable if you are planning to rent a car in Orlando.

> *Tip:* The easiest way to do this is by using the web site, www.itasoftware.com. It allows you to search fares from any given airport to another, plus alternatives with "x" miles. Start with alternative airports within reasonable driving distance from your home. Then look into service from those airports to both Orlando International and a few Florida alternatives. The main ones are:

> *Sanford.* About a 45-minute drive from Disney World, Sanford is popular with charter airlines. Disney offers a one-way shuttle from the Sanford Airport for around $20 per person. Call Disney at 407-934-7639 (W-Disney) to book. It might be cheaper to rent a car for the drive.

> *Tampa.* A little over an hour away from WDW, the Tampa airport is close to Interstate 4. You can take I-4 straight to the entrance of Disney World.

> *Melbourne.* About an hour and a half from Disney World, this airport is near the beach. You could fly in and go to the beach on your first day of vacation and then drive on to Orlando that night or the next morning.

> *Jacksonville.* Over two hours north of Disney, this could be an option for those who have extra time and want to see the surrounding area.

> *Note:* This strategy might work out for you even if you don't plan drive while you are in Orlando. Check the cost of renting a car just to drive between the alternate airport and your hotel. (Remember, you'll need to do it both ways.) If the total cost for your air tickets plus the car rentals represents a good savings over the cost of air-

fare directly to Orlando, it may be worth the extra hassle.

• **Check the airlines' own web sites** and sign up for bulletins on their latest deals. Do not depend on travel web sites like Expedia or Travelocity to find the best fare on a flight. Check the major airlines' web sites for deals you can't find anywhere else. If you live in an area that has several regional airlines, be sure to check their sites as well. Many times the smaller, regional players do not show up at all on the big travel sites. Look around and do your home-work.

Note: You can register with most airlines and they will let you know when a good deal comes out. Some will even tell you when your particular destination becomes available at a discount.

Airlines that serve Orlando

These airlines offer service to Orlando International Airport (MCO):

• **Major U.S. airlines**

American Airlines - www.aa.com

Continental Airlines - www.flycontinental.com

Delta - www.delta.com

Northwest Airlines - www.nwa.com

Southwest Airlines - www.southwest.com

United - www.united.com

US Airways - www.usairways.com

• **Regional and low-fare U.S. airlines**

Air Tran - www.airtran.com

Alaska Airlines - www.alaskaair.com

America West Airlines - www.americawest.com

Frontier - www.frontierairlines.com

Independence Air - www.flyi.com

Jet Blue - www.jetblue.com

Song - www.flysong.com

Spirit Airlines - www.spiritair.com

Sun Country Airlines - www.suncountry.com

Ted - www.flyted.com

USA 3000 - www.usa3000.com

• **Canadian airlines**

Air Canada - www.aircanada.ca

CanJet - www.canjet.com

Airlines that serve nearby Sanford

Allegiant Air - www.allegiantair.com

Pan Am - www.flypanam.com

TransMeridian - www.iflytma.com

Vacation Express - www.vacationexpress.com

• **Which airport is right for you?** Many individuals are lucky and have many, many options when it comes to picking the best airport and getting the best flight. If you are one of those lucky ones, you might be able to fly to Disney World instead of drive. Markets like New York, Baltimore, Boston, Burbank (CA), Chicago, Detroit, Lansing (MI), Los Angeles, New Jersey, Oakland, Ontario (Canada), and Rhode Island have at least four airports within 100 miles. If you live in these markets, you are more likely to find a good deal than you'll find if you live in a one-airport community.

To know what your options are, look at www.alternateairports.com. This site has most of the major (and minor) airports and a list of airports that are relatively close to them. It is important to understand your options. It could be well worth it to spending an extra hour driving to the airport to save several hundred dollars on your flight. When you know your options and how far you are willing to drive, research fares at www.itasoftware.com and see what is the best fit for you. You can reserve offsite parking (usually cheaper) at the airport of your choice online at www.airportparkingreservations.com.

Consult Some Travel Agents Before Booking

Search all of the web sites, find the best deal, and then call a travel agent to see if they can beat it. Travel agents often have access to better deals than you can get on your own. This isn't always the case, but it doesn't hurt or cost anything to ask. Remember, travel agents work for you, generally for free. They are compensated by the hotels, rental car companies, and so on that they book for you. (The airlines, however, now stiff them, which is why some travel agents may charge you a fee if you want them to research air tickets for you.)

Of course, a travel agent may not have the best deal for you, especially if they do not specialize in Disney, because a lot of agents concentrate on convenience instead of affordability. Based on our personal experiences, travel agents who don't specialize in Disney World travel don't know all of the details involved in booking a "cost savings" package. For example, the ones we tried pushed the "Disney Package" as the only way to book and stay onsite. Even when they added in discounted airfare and free shuttle service, the package was still over-priced because they didn't understand the various options and therefore led clients to believe that they had to buy the whole package to get the options they wanted. In fairness to the agents, they may have believed this themselves. But that's no help to their clients.

Look for a Disney specialist. If you want to take the hassle out of booking your own trip and finding the best deal, we highly recommend that you use a travel agent who specializes in Disney World travel. Such an agent is typically more knowledgeable about WDW and understands the value that their customers are looking for. A Disney specialist will be up to date on all of the latest deals from Disney and will know of any financial benefits to be gained by bundling services.

A Disney specialist should meet the following criteria:

- The majority of their business should be focused on Disney.
- They should be willing to customize packages and should be very familiar with the different resorts and accommodations at WDW.
- They should be willing to book offsite accommodations for you.

Use a travel agent who guarantees you the lowest price and is willing to change your reservations if new specials from Disney come out. The agent should continually seek out the best deal and apply any and all discounts that come along. They should do this even after you book your vacation. For example, if the best price for a room at the time of booking was $99 a night, and a special for $77 a night came out a couple of months later, the agent should apply the $22 a night savings back to your account. That way you will never have to worry about booking at the wrong time or wonder if you got the best deal. Better yet, you don't have to continually hunt for the specials; they do all the work for you!

Magical Journeys, Kingdom Konsultants, Mouse Ear Vacations, Small World Vacations, and Second Star Vacations are among the travel agencies that specialize in Disney vacations. Not only do they specialize in Disney vacations, but also they are very price conscious and understand how important it is for people to save money. All five are highly reputable, easy to work with, and dedicated to helping individuals experience the best Disney has to offer. They will see to it that you get the best possible deal.

You can contact these Disney specialists at their web sites:

>www.yourmagicaljourneys.com
>www.kingdomkonsultants.com
>www.mouseearvacations.com
>www.wdwvacations.com
>www.secondstarvacations.com

Tell them *Disney on a Dime* sent you!

In the *Introduction*, we offered an example of a budget for a four-day, five-night trip in which our family (of four then) went to WDW for under $1,400. Opposite is an example of how much we saved compared with the WDW package various non-specialist travel agents offered us at the time. We've updated the ticket cost to reflect 2005 prices. (And we know now that we needed to find an agent who specialized in Disney vacations.)

Use Frequent Flyer Miles

We've known several families who have traveled to Disney World for free by using the frequent flyer miles they have earned on their business travel. Many companies allow employees to keep the travel miles they earn. If yours is one of them, and you are allowed to choose the carrier for your business trips, try to use the same airline consistently. If you do not do so, your miles could be spread out over several carriers and you might not earn enough miles on any one of them to qualify for any free tickets.

>*Note:* Be sure that the airline you use offers service to Orlando or
>has a partner that does.

You can also build personal frequent flyer mileage:

• **Use credit cards that award miles for purchases**. Many people earn a lot of mileage by using these cards to pay for most of their regular purchases — groceries, gas, utility bills, tuition, and so on. If you go this route, remember to pay off the balance each month so that you don't incur finance charges.

• **Look for other programs that offer free miles.** Many airlines offer miles for booking online or for renting a car. Check their sites and other travel sites for the most up-to-date information.

>*Caution:* You could also check eBay for frequent flyer miles or
>vouchers for sale. However, we advise against this. It is a high-

High Way vs. Our Way			
Expense	**Package**	**Our Way**	**Savings**
Travel	Fly $250 per ticket	Drive $200 for gas	$800
Hotel/Food en route*	(not applicable)	$100	[- $100]
Tickets	$1,191 (Premier tkts + tax)	$710 (Base tkts + tax)	$481
Hotel	$99/night (Value onsite)	$32/night (offsite)	$335
Food	$100/day for Dining Plan $50/day for snacks	$18/day all meals in hotel room $7.50/day for snacks	$488 $170
Souvenirs	$100 total ($25/person)	$40 total ($10/person)	$60
Total	**$3,546**	**$1,312**	**$2,234**

*Note: We normally drive straight through to Orlando (18 hours), without an overnight stop. But we've added one in to give a better comparison for those who prefer to drive fewer hours a day or who live too far away to drive straight through.

risk strategy that could cost you your vacation. The airlines have threatened to sue people who try to use vouchers they haven't earned. And they have made some passengers they've caught in the act pay the full price for their tickets.

When You Land in Orlando You're Not There Yet

You'll have to arrange to get from the airport to WDW or your offsite hotel and back if you fly. That will be easy if you are staying at a WDW resort and plan to spend all your time on Disney property. If not, your options are renting a car or using a limo or outside shuttle service. These are expenses you wouldn't have if you chose to drive.

• **Disney's Magical Express airport shuttle.** If you're staying at WDW any time before November 2006, Disney will shuttle you to and from Orlando International Airport and look after your bags. You won't even have to hang around to pick them up from the baggage carousel. Disney will take care of that and deliver them directly to your Resort room. This is a great service that allows Disney Resort guests to start and end their vacation in a magical way.

Magical Express service is free through 2006 in conjunction with Disney's "Happiest Celebration on Earth" (May 2005 through October 2006). After that, it will probably cost if it is continued, but presumably the cost would be competitive with other shuttles that serve the airport.

Note: As long as it remains free, this service is a fantastic money-saver and could be a viable reason to stay onsite. The service will save a family of four (two adults and two children under age fourteen) $100 in normal shuttle/transportation fees. You can apply this savings to the overall cost of staying onsite. If you are staying for five nights, this gives you an extra $20 a night. If a room at a Value Resort costs $77 a night and a room offsite would cost $50, it might be a better deal to stay onsite after you figure in the savings and convenience of the free shuttle service.

> *Caution:* If you want to see more of Orlando than Disney World, you may want to rent a car anyway. Taxis to and from WDW are prohibitively expensive for most people and not that easy to find.

• **Public shuttle services.** A typical shuttle or van service charges on a per-person basis. The going round-trip rate is around $30 per adult and $20 per child (ages 4 to 11; under 4 free). Note that this is not an individual service like a taxi or a limo. You share the shuttle van with others going to different places. You may be the first stop or the fifth; it all depends on who gets on with you. If you go this route, the best-known service is probably Mears (1-407-423-5566).

> *Tip:* If you have four people (either four adults or a mix of adults and children) in your party, you could take a taxi or limo service for the price of a shuttle service.

• **Cabs.** A cab will charge a flat rate of at least $80 round-trip for one to four people. Most cabs will allow a stop at a grocery store for an additional fee. Take advantage of it. It can save you a lot more than the $15 to $20 it costs on the meter (see below).

• **Limos**. A limo service will cost around $100 roundtrip. Like cab fare, this is a flat rate that does not fluctuate with the number of passengers. Up to four, or sometimes five, may ride for that price. Most companies will allow a complimentary stop at a grocery store on the way to your hotel.

> *Tip:* If you plan to take advantage of the free stop — and we strongly recommend that you do — the price of limo service becomes very competitive with cab service and even more convenient because you can reserve it before you leave home.

One company that we have been very satisfied with is QuickSilver limo service. They offer roundtrip service from the airport to your hotel and back again. Every trip comes with a complementary 30-minute grocery stop, free long-distance/international phone calls, free car seats, and a gift. They try their best to have the same driver for your trips to and from the airport. Their vehicles include town cars, luxury SUVs, limos, and vans. A typical trip in a town car would run under $100 roundtrip for one to four people.

> *Note:* QuickSilver suggests that big groups (five to ten people) get a van. The charge will be a little over $100. This is a great deal for families and groups when compared to taking Mears or a taxi. You'll find them on the web at www.quicksilvertours.com and by phone at 1-888-GO-TO-WDW. Tell them you read about them in *Disney on a Dime.*

• **Rental cars**. Sometimes it can be cheaper to rent a car. If you are just staying for the weekend, look at the very low rates many car rental companies offer. A rental car might be as inexpensive as $12 per weekend day, and most rental car companies define weekend days as Friday, Saturday, and Sunday. We rented a car from a Thursday afternoon to a Sunday afternoon on one trip for a total of $65. This was cheaper than using any of the other transportation alternatives, and we had the bonus of always having access to a car.

> *$$aver Tip:* There is a cheap way to get to WDW that is open to anyone, but it is a long trip. You can take the public bus system from Orlando International to Disney World. The bus doesn't come by often and the total trip could take several hours, because the bus will make all of its regular stops along the way. If you're game anyway, you can use the "Online Bus Trip Planner" at www.golynx.com.

A Fly / Drive Cost Comparison

If you are within reasonable driving distance of Disney World, be sure to calculate the potential savings that driving can bring. The table below gives a rough example of the comparative costs of flying and driving from some major markets within driving distance of Orlando.

Traveling from:	Flying			Driving	Potential Savings
	Shuttle to hotel	Per person	Family of 4	25 mpg $2.50/gal	
Atlanta	$100	$181	$824	$90	$734
Chicago	$100	$150	$700	$250	$450
Cincinnati	$100	$200	$900	$188	$712
Dallas	$100	$250	$1,100	$238	$862
Kansas City	$100	$200	$900	$269	$631
New Orleans	$100	$150	$700	$138	$562
New York*	$100	$150	$700	$250	$450

*The New York area has access to many discounted flights, some as low as $100 R/T.

Here's what we included in our calculations:

For flying: the average cost of a round-trip ticket plus a shuttle from the Orlando airport to an offsite hotel. If you plan to rent a car, it will usually cost more. (We did not include the cost of getting to and from your departure airport.) Keep in mind that airline ticket prices fluctuate. If you plan diligently, you may be able to find tickets or alternate airports that offer significant savings.

For driving: fuel costs of $2.50 per gallon times distance for a vehicle that gets 25 miles per gallon, or mpg. (We did not include food, drinks, or a possible hotel stay, but even when you add them in, you can see that driving offers substantial savings.)

Study your particular situation and needs before deciding which makes more sense for you and your family. Be sure to consider all the factors we've already discussed, including the value of your time, before making a final decision.

Taking a Bus

If you do not mind a long trip, taking a bus could be an inexpensive alternative to flying or driving. Bus travel is not as common as it used to be, but it is still there and it is still a viable way to save money.

Greyhound is the biggest and most popular bus line, and it serves the entire U.S. It is common for Greyhound to offer great specials that allow 50% off round-trip tickets or that allow a guest to ride for free.

The biggest downside to taking a bus is the time involved. If it normally takes 15 hours to drive to Disney World, expect it to take around 22 hours by bus. The other downside is getting from the Greyhound terminal at 555 North John Young Parkway in downtown Orlando to Disney World. One option is to take Lynx bus number 303 to the Downtown Disney West Side Transfer Center, but that is a long ride. There are several rental car companies within a mile of the terminal including Enterprise (407-578-2722), Budget (407-298-9995), U Save (407-445-1516), and Hertz (407-521-4154). Taxi fares will be higher than from the airport.

For Greyhound's rates, schedules, and bus stops along the way, check out www.greyhound.com.

Extra Travel Tips from "Disney on a Dime"

Have an infant? Bring a car. The transportation system at Walt Disney World is very efficient and will suffice for most as a replacement to having your own vehicle — unless you have an infant or very small child. An infant who needs to eat, get a diaper change, or go to sleep cannot wait 10 minutes for the bus to come and then another 15 to 20 minutes to get back to the hotel room. Twenty to thirty minutes with a screaming child is stressful for everyone, the child, the parents, and everyone else on the bus, and the wait and journey can be even longer at the end of the day when the parks close. Depending on where you are and where you are going, getting from park to park can take 30 to 45 minutes at any time of the day and also strain you and your child.

If you have a car, you can quickly get the little one into the comfort of air-conditioning and a car seat, and then back to the hotel room in a matter of minutes. Consider renting a car if you don't drive to Disney World.

Note: The car also comes in handy for carting a stroller and extra supplies of diapers, formula, and baby food to the parks with you.

Look into buying travel insurance. Due to the extreme weather changes that can occur in the Orlando area, it could be a good investment to consider getting travel insurance. Contact your insurance provider or travel agencies that offer this coverage. The coverage could be much less than you think. If you book your flight through Travelocity or another online service, insurance runs between $15 and $25 per person.

If you are going to travel during the hurricane season (June to October), you are taking a risk that your vacation could easily be wiped out by a storm.

Caution: Comparison shop carefully and examine the fine print to make sure any insurance you get covers what you want it to cover.

Travel during the "off-season." If your schedule permits, try to travel outside of the typical spring break, summer, and holiday times. You are bound to have a less stressful vacation if you go at less popular times of the year. If you drive, there will typically be fewer cars on the road than during peak travel seasons. If you are flying, you will find cheaper airfares and may have more room on the plane to stretch out. Being able to find a cheap hotel room is also a plus.

Other advantages include shorter lines in the parks, milder weather, deep discounts from Disney, uncrowded hotel pools, and easier access to restaurants. Don't get caught in the herd at Disney World if you can help it.

Sign up for emails from hotel chains. Many popular hotel chains offer email alerts when they run specials and discounts on rooms. Very nice hotel chains like Marriott and Hilton regularly discount their hotel rooms by 50% or more. Subscribe to these alerts and check their web sites before your trip. If you are driving, you could get a great deal at a nice hotel along the way.

Don't pay for long-distance calls. Always look for 1-800 numbers when calling about a hotel, flight, or transportation. Most companies have them, but a lot of them make you look for it. So you may have to dig a little. Look up the company on the Internet. If the company doesn't have a web site, try www.switchboard.com. Or call 1-800-555-1212, the toll-free directory service.

If a toll-free number is not available, try to call on a cell phone during your "free minutes." Most cell phones now come with free nights and weekends. Call during these times for free. Most establishments have someone to talk to at all hours of the day and night. Take advantage of this.

Tip: If you don't need to call, don't. Most companies have inter-active web sites that allow you to search, reserve, pay for, and confirm services without ever needing to talk to anyone.

Buy a package. If you are researching airfares, try additional searches to find out what you might save by buying a package that combines airfare and lodging (and perhaps a rental car, as well). Most travel web sites offer deep discounts for such packages. We've found Expedia a good source for pack-ages that include a stay at a WDW Resort hotel, while Travelocity is good for packages that include offsite hotels.

Recently we were able to stay virtually for free by buying such a package. Our quoted airfare was $272 (without a hotel). By adding a three-night hotel stay and buying it as a package with our airfare, we got both for a total cost of $264 — $8 less than we would have paid for airfare alone if we had booked our hotel separately. (If we had wanted to stay only two nights, the total price would have been $252 with the hotel.) Try out different scenarios and find the best and cheapest that works for you.

$$aver Tip: Look at flying and the possible savings that could be achieved by buying an air-lodging package even if you are plan-ning to drive. The potential savings may make you change your plans. Just be sure to include the cost of getting to and from the airports in your calculations. And keep in mind that really good deals aren't usually available at Christmas time.

Note: If you are looking for a discount on WDW rooms with-out buying an air-hotel package, be aware that WDW is the only source.

Check package deals from AAA. AAA is a sponsor of Disney World and offers some great Disney World deals to their members. Check with them and then compare their packages to what others advertise or to what you can put together yourself.

$$aver Tip: AAA offers a great parking pass that can be used on Disney property. The "Triple Diamond" pass allows its holders to go to the front of the parking lot where a group of reserved spaces are located. Be warned that these spaces are limited and can fill up very quickly. When they're gone, they're gone.

Shop around and then shop some more. Unfortunately, a lot of times if you want to find that good deal, you have to work hard for it by doing your homework and looking around. There are some great deals out there for airfare, rental cars, and overall travel expenses; you just have to put a little sweat equity into finding them.

When you are looking, make lists of the different deals that you find and how long the offer is available. Don't pull the trigger on the first deal that you see. Chances are there is a better offer out there. Use the different travel and airline web sites before booking.

Give your travel budget some breathing room. Round up on some of your estimates to help cover unforeseen expenses. For example, gas prices could go up during your trip. In some months in the recent past, gas prices have gone up as much as 45 cents a gallon over a two-week period. In fact, it happened during our last trip to Disney World. Sites such as www.gasbuddy.com and www.orlandogasprices.com can help you track price trends before you leave. That won't change the price, but at least you'll know what to expect.

Your flight might be delayed, necessitating unexpected food purchases to keep your family fed and happy while you wait. If you've budgeted a little extra, you won't have to worry about blowing your vacation funds.

Getting into the Disney "Mood" on the Road

You don't have to wait until you get to Disney World to get into the Disney spirit. Disney music, books, and movies can really put you in a magical mood while you're on the way.

Disney Music

Great collections of Disney music can be found at the Disney Store and local discount shops. Listening to them is a great way to stay in the Disney mood during the trip down and back. On the trip down, the music helps build anticipation. On the trip home, it can spark recent memories of the parks and the Disney atmosphere. And if you drive while at the parks, keep the spirit alive with the constant sound of Disney in the car.

Look for Disney World CDs that have music from the rides, shows, pavilions, and fireworks. You can buy them at the parks or plan ahead and look on eBay.

Disney Books and Coloring Books

Take along "The Walt Disney World Trivia Book," by Louis Mongello. It's filled with fun multiple-choice questions about Disney World. You'll not only have fun guessing at the answers, but also learn a lot of secrets and fun facts.

You can pick up inexpensive Disney books and coloring books at almost any discount store. Or print coloring pages off the Internet at many sites, including ours: www.disneyonadime.com. Alternatively, look into an inexpensive computer program that will give you everything you need to produce your own.

Disney Movies

Mobile DVD or video cassette players cost under $200 and can be used after (and before) your Disney trip. Consider getting one to prep the kids for what lies ahead. Try to pick movies that have a corresponding ride or show at Disney World, such as *Peter Pan, Winnie the Pooh, Snow White, The Lion King, Pirates of the Caribbean, The Little Mermaid,* or *Beauty and the Beast.* This is a great way to pump the kids (and adults) up about what they are about to see, and it will help them identify the characters when they are in the parks.

Or bring a laptop computer with a built-in DVD player. If you use this option, be sure to put extra batteries in the glove compartment or invest in a $20 converter that will let you plug your laptop into the cigarette lighter.

- Start with a Cooler

- Breakfast

- Snacks & Beverages in the Parks

- Lunch & Dinner

- The Disney Dining Experience Card

- Extra Tips

SAVE ON FOOD & DRINK

Food and drink can really "eat" into your vacation budget. When you eat out three meals a day plus snacks, the food bill skyrockets — especially when you're feeding a family. Yet people often underestimate the amount they need to budget for food on vacation. This chapter will help you keep your vacation food budget both realistic and as low as possible for the kind of vacation eating you prefer.

Before we offer detailed tips and tricks for keeping the budget down, keep this in mind. To save on food in general, eat as many meals as possible outside the theme parks. To save the maximum amount, eat meals you prepare in your hotel room and bring in the food and drinks you'll eat in the theme parks in a cooler.

There is absolutely nothing wrong with eating meals in your hotel room and brown bagging your theme-park meals. Most people do it for at least some of their meals, and it is by far the best way to save money on your overall food budget.

If you are driving to Disney World, following this advice will be easy. Just pack your car and cooler with the food you'll need (see "Kitchen and On-the-Road Meal Items," *Chapter Ten* for suggestions). If you're flying to Disney, you'll need to do a little more planning (see "Hungry?" below).

> *Note:* "Budget Eating" in no way diminishes the value or magic of a trip to Disney World; most visitors don't go there for the food. You won't miss out by not eating in the theme parks. However, if you prefer to eat out for some (or all) of your meals or you want to enjoy a Character Meal with your kids, we'll suggest economical ways to do those things, too. The choices are yours to make.

Start with a Cooler — Maybe Two

You will save a lot on food by packing your own to eat in the theme parks instead of buying all your meals at the theme park restaurants and counter-service establishments. You'll need to pack your food and drinks in a cooler that you can leave in a park locker until you want it. While the official line from Disney is that outside food is not allowed inside the parks, we've never had a problem bringing it in. In fact, cast members (Disney's name for its employees) at the gates may praise you for having the foresight and smarts to bring your own food.

> *Note:* We especially recommend packing a cooler if you plan to drive to Disney World. Fill it full of drinks, snacks, and food for the road to save the cost of buying those items at pricey rest stops along the way.

> *Tip:* If your hotel room isn't equipped with a refrigerator (see *Chapters Seven* and *Eight*), you may want to bring two coolers, one for the room and one for the parks.

Thirsty?

Everybody needs water during a day of walking around the WDW theme parks, but bottled water and soft drinks cost $2.50 each in the parks. This is probably OK for an occasional drink, but most people need three to four a day to stay hydrated in the warm Florida sun. Do the math: you could spend a fortune unnecessarily.

Here are some ways to make sure you don't spend a fortune quenching your thirst. Potential savings: up to $200 per week for a family of four.

Water

Go to a grocery store before your first visit to the theme parks and buy cases of bottled water plus a small insulated cooler to take with you into the parks. Keep the water bottles on ice in a cooler or in your hotel refrigerator if your room has one. If you have a freezer in the fridge, freeze a couple of bottles and use them to keep the others cool during the day.

Bring one canteen or water bottle into the park for each member of your party. The WDW counter-service restaurants will refill them with water and ice for free. Or refill them yourself at a water fountain. (Fountains are abundant wherever restrooms are found.) If the sulfurous taste of Orlando's water gets to you (as it does to us), you can purchase portable water filters and bring them with you. Better yet, get refillable water bottles with a built-in water filter. They cost around $8 and are very effective in improving the taste. If you don't want to splurge for a water filter, try water-purifying tablets. You will find them in the camping section of most discount stores.

> *$$aver Tip:* Cups of ice are free at WDW parks. You may want to get them just to munch on the ice. Ice, by itself, can be a nice relief in the heat of the summer. Cups of ice water are also free. Ask for free ice water anytime you are thirsty. If you buy a meal at a theme park restaurant, order ice water with your meal to save paying for a drink.

Other options for your water:

• **Use insulated carriers for your water bottles.** They do a good job of keeping the water colder longer. They normally come with a strap and are comfortable to carry around. You'll find them in discount stores. Or,

• **Bring backpacks equipped with "bladders"** (built-in water containers). They hold a liter and a half (or more) of liquid and have a drinking tube that comes out of the top. You can drink from the tube as you walk, just like you'd do with a straw. Camelbak is one manufacturer of these devices. Discount stores such as Target carry more generic brands, but our experience is that these tend to leak.

Juice

Bring in juice boxes for young children in a backpack. Use plastic sandwich bags filled with ice from your hotel or "Blue Ice" packs kept cold in a refrigerator to keep them at a desirable temperature.

Soda

If you must have a soft drink, you can bring in a few cans in your cooler or splurge on an occasional soda at a counter-service restaurant. Here are some ways to save on park purchases:

• **Ask for little or no ice when you buy a soda.** The fountain soda is already cold, and you'll get more for your money.

• **Buy one large cup of soda and ask for an extra cup** with or without ice. Then share the soda with a friend or family member.

• **Refillable resort mugs.** The Disney resorts sell insulated mugs that entitle you to free water or soda refills during your stay. This is a good deal if you insist on buying soft drinks at the resorts rather than at the grocery store. After a couple of refills, they pay for themselves.

> *Caution:* The refills are only good at the resort where you are staying. They do not qualify for free refills inside the theme parks.

• **Enjoy FREE sodas at Ice Station Cool in Epcot.** This refreshment center, which may be renamed Club Cool by the time you visit, is sponsored by Coca-Cola. It lets you sample soft drinks from around the world. Little paper cups are provided at various help-yourself fountains around the room. If you aren't up for possibly swallowing an odd-tasting cola, don't try this. Some of the drinks are delicious; while others are quite, well, different. This is a chance to quench your thirst free, though. You can drink as much as you want — or as much as your taste buds can handle, whichever comes first. Ice Station Cool is located beside Innovations East and the water fountain at Millennium Central. Look for an entrance that looks like an iceberg. You'll enjoy the air conditioning, too.

Hungry?

The wonderful smells of cooking food in the theme parks will tempt your taste buds! The important decision is whether or not you want to spend a lot of money on table-service restaurants, somewhat less money on counter-service food, or eat outside of the parks and have more to spend on things like souvenirs. What will your family remember: eating in an upscale restaurant or getting to have ice cream during the fireworks?

As we said at the beginning of this chapter, our biggest tip for saving on food is to eat as many meals outside the parks as possible — especially meals you can prepare in your hotel room. If you are flying to Disney, here some options for getting that food:

• **Pack and carry snacks in your suitcase.** Pack nonperishable snacks in plastic Sterilite® or Rubbermaid® containers that will fit inside your suitcase. That way, snacks won't get crushed.

• **Pack and send snacks to your hotel.** Pack up your nonperishable snacks and mail them to your resort or hotel a few days before your arrival. Call ahead and ask if this is OK. Most hotels will let you do it. Get instructions from them on how to address and label the package. Also, find out if they will charge you a handling fee.

• **Have groceries delivered to your hotel.** Some online grocery outlets such as www.netgrocer.com will ship groceries to any location. This could be an inexpensive money saver. You could even have groceries delivered twice during your stay, on your first day and then later in your stay.

If you're staying in or near Walt Disney World, you may want to order online from Goodings, a grocery store close to Disney World that delivers to most hotels and resorts in the area. Goodings has a minimum order amount of $50 and charges $10 for delivery as we go to press. For the latest information, check its web site, www.goodings.com.

• **Pick up the groceries yourself.** Limos and many taxis allow a 30-minute grocery stop between the airport and your destination. Ask your driver if you can have one, and be sure to have your grocery list handy so that you can make best use of your time. If you have a car at your disposal, you'll pass plenty of grocery stores on the way to your hotel. Or ask someone at your hotel's front desk for directions to the nearest grocery or discount store if you are staying off property.

The following stores are most convenient to WDW. Consult Mapquest (www.mapquest.com) for driving directions:

> Publix
> 2915 Vineland Road
> Kissimmee 34746
>
> Publix
> 3972 Town Center Boulevard
> Orlando 32837
>
> Wal-Mart Supercenter
> 4444 West Vine Street
> Kissimmee 34746
>
> Sam's Club
> 4763 West Irlo Bronson Highway
> Kissimmee 34746

Breakfast

• **Go for the free breakfast.** If you plan to stay in a hotel outside of WDW, try to find one that serves a free breakfast. That would be one "free" meal each day of your vacation! If the breakfast includes fruits, such as bananas or apples, you can also take a few pieces (don't be greedy!) to eat as snacks later in the day. We can't stress this enough. Demand the free meal and you will save.

• **Make your own breakfast.** If you stay at Disney World or in another hotel or resort that does not offer a free breakfast, bring your own breakfast food to enjoy in your room. Buy bagels, donuts, and other breakfast pastries, fruit, dry cereal, granola, or bread and jam ahead of time. If you have a room with a fridge, bring along cream cheese, butter, small containers of juice, and milk. If you don't have a fridge, consider keeping these things on ice. This requires a little work each day, dumping water out of the cooler and putting in fresh ice, but it pays off in big savings and gives you a nicer variety of breakfast options.

• **The coffee maker isn't just for coffee.** Use the coffee maker in your room to heat water to make warm foods, such as instant oatmeal, hot chocolate, and soup.

See *Chapters Six* and *Eight*, for more money-saving tips on eating in your hotel room.

Snacks and Beverages for the Parks

You don't have to buy food and beverages in the theme parks. In fact, the security people who examine bags at WDW have often congratulated us for our foresight in bringing snacks and drinks.

• **Stash them in a park locker.** Pack a big backpack or medium-sized collapsible cooler with snacks, sandwiches, and drinks and store it in a park locker (they're approximately 18 inches high by 12 inches wide). When you need to grab a bite, simply go to your cooler. The lockers cost $5 a day plus a $2 deposit.

> *Tip:* The great thing about the lockers is that the rental is portable from park to park throughout the day. Return your key to the service desk and they will return your $2 and a voucher for same-day use at another WDW park. Simply take the voucher to another park that day, give them a $2 deposit, and you will receive a new locker.

• **Snacks are a must,** especially if you have small children in your family. Remember, your children's regular snacks are probably not available inside the parks. Bring your children's favorite cookies, crackers, or even yogurt. Fed children are happy children! Here are some ideas for economical, easy-to-carry snacks:

> *Pack* trail mix, snack crackers, fruit, or granola bars in a backpack and

snack while standing in line or strolling around the parks.

Buy enough small canisters of Pringles® chips for everyone in your group. When the chips are gone, save the small canisters and refill them with chips (or other snacks) from a full size container. The canisters travel well in a bag, as they do not crush easily.

Fix sandwiches in your hotel room and carry them in a plastic container. We like the sandwich-sized plastic Gladware® containers that you can buy at any grocery store. They are great for taking sandwiches into the park because they stack well in a backpack or other bag. You can also use them to carry snack crackers or snack mix. They come in a variety of sizes.

• **Cheap snacks in the parks.** Fruit is about the most inexpensive snack Disney offers. Most pieces cost just a dollar or two. You'll find them at snack kiosks located throughout the parks. Some stands also offer cut-up fruits (like melon) and fruit salad. Other great inexpensive snacks include ice cream and ice pops, pretzels, popcorn, and turkey legs.

$$aver Tip: Be careful to limit your snack stops if you are buying your snacks in the parks. While $3 for an ice cream sounds relatively inexpensive, multiply it by a number of people and it adds up fast. Consider making such purchases special events rather than everyday treats.

Lunch and Dinner, In and Out

Need we repeat that you can eat lunch and dinner outside the parks for much, much less than you'd spend inside? Of course, it can be fun to treat yourself to a special meal, and some people don't feel like they're on vacation unless they eat out. The choices are yours to make. Just be sure to budget appropriately.

Here are some tips for saving on lunch and dinner whether you choose to make them yourself, buy them offsite, or pay for Disney fare.

• **Eat — and rest — in your room.** If you hit the parks in the morning when they open and snack throughout the time you are there, take a break around 1:00 or 2:00 p.m. Go back to your hotel to rest and put the little ones down for a nap. Lunch in your room, before or after the naps. When you are all fed and the kids are rested, hit the parks again, energized and ready to take on the late afternoon with rides and attractions you didn't get to earlier in the day. Your children will enjoy the nighttime shows much more with that nap under their belts. As you look around in the evenings, it will be easy to spot the families that didn't take a break. Many of the children in those families will be screaming, irritable, or asleep during the fireworks.

• **What's for lunch, Mom?** Sandwiches are easiest. Bring in bread, peanut butter, jelly, ham and cheese, packets of condiments, chips, and cookies for a light, yet filling lunch in the comfort of your hotel room. You'll save big bucks because you won't be eating out. And you'll find the peace and quiet a nice change of pace after a busy morning in the parks.

• **Tailgate.** For another change of pace, or if your hotel room is too far away from the parks to make the trip back and forth worthwhile, try tailgating instead. It's good enough for the football game and it's good enough for Disney World. Bring an efficient cooler with you to the parks and leave it in your vehicle. Pack it with all that you'll need to make sandwiches or prepare a meal that suits you. If it's hot, you can sit in the car and cool off in the air-conditioning as you eat. If the weather is good, hang out in the parking lot or find a nice shade tree to sit under and have a picnic. Then let the little ones rest for a bit before heading back into the park.

> *Note:* There's nothing wrong with tailgating on the Disney World properties. Just don't try setting up a grill. That's not allowed for safety reasons.

• **What's for dinner, Dad?** We've put together sample menus of items you can fix in your hotel room with or without a microwave. See *Chapter Nine.*

• **Order from the dollar menu at offsite fast food restaurants.** If you are staying offsite, you are almost certain to find several fast food restaurants in the vicinity of your hotel. Eating there is cheaper than eating in Disney World, even at WDW counter-service places. A cheap way to feed your family at a fast food place would be to go to the drive-thru and order off of the $1 menu. Just order a burger and fries for everyone. Remember, you already have drinks in the cooler or refrigerator back at the hotel. A family of four can make a meal of fast food for under $9.00.

> *Note:* The McDonald's restaurants located on Disney property do not offer a $1 menu.

• **Order a la carte from WDW counter-service restaurants.** Most people don't realize that their options at these restaurants aren't limited to what is displayed on the restaurant's menu board. Most menus list combos — a burger and fries, for example — but do not list the items individually. You do not need to order the combo to get the item you want. For example, if you only want the burger and don't care for the fries, ask them to take the fries off and then ask what the new price would be. Using this technique will lower your food bill, as well as saving you from paying for something you don't want.

• **Silly Rabbit, kid's meals aren't just for kids.** Adults can order kids' meals for themselves (at counter-service restaurants only) and fill up for less. The portions are big enough for an adult and cost, on average, two dollars less than an adult meal (under $4 for a kid's hamburger platter, for example, versus nearly $6 for an adult platter). In addition, the kid's meal comes with a drink and the adult meal doesn't, so you will get more for your buck. You may also waste less food and save a few calories.

• **Have two meals in one with a late Character Breakfast.** Book the latest seating and your meal can double as lunch. If your children are dying for a Character Meal, schedule a Character Breakfast at the latest available time. Most Character Breakfasts have final seating close to 11 a.m. Cinderella's Royal Table, however, seats its last guests at 11:15 a.m., which lets them eat until around noon or a bit later — thus making the meal a "brunch." Most Character Meals are buffets, so you can eat to your heart's content and should be quite satisfied until dinnertime. Budget about $21.99 per adult and $11.99 per child (nine and under) plus tax.

> *Note:* To make this strategy work for you, eat a snack in the morning. Then go to the park where the breakfast is to be served (the Magic Kingdom for Cinderella's Royal Table) and ride the rides till it's time to eat.

> *Tip:* The Character Breakfast at Cinderella's Royal Table is immensely popular. You must make advance reservations. We highly recommended that you call exactly 90 days before the date you desire. Call at 7:00 a.m. Eastern time and keep calling until you get in. This is one of the hardest reservations to get at Walt Disney World.

• **Eat a late lunch instead of dinner** to save at WDW sit-down restaurants. If you eat "dinner" at the tail end of the restaurant's lunch service, you can often get the same food for less because the lunch price of a given item is frequently cheaper than the dinner price. In addition to saving money, you'll have the pleasure of dining when the restaurant is less crowded.

> *Tip:* If you decide to eat dinner or lunch in the parks, avoid typical meal times. Eat a little early or a little late to dodge the massive crowds. You'll not only have a more enjoyable meal, but also

enjoy shorter lines for the rides and attractions while others are lining up for tables.

• **Take advantage of Annual Passholder discounts if you can.** Some WDW sit-down restaurants give Passholder discounts. The discount is generally 10% and is offered during the lunch hours. It usually covers the Passholder and three additional guests. These benefits change from time to time, so be sure to check your Annual Passholder benefits guide for the latest offerings and participating restaurants.

• **Babies need food, too.** Don't forget the babies! There are nursing and bottle warming stations in all of the parks. Check your park maps for locations. These are nice places to rest and tend to your little ones. You'll find many other places in WDW to discreetly nurse little ones, but if you'd like some place quiet, the baby stations are comfortable.

• **Make advance reservations for sit-down meals at WDW.** Many Disney World sit-down restaurants are very popular. If you want to eat dinner at one of them, be sure to make advance reservations. We'd recommend you do it weeks, if not months, before your vacation if your family is looking forward to eating in a particular place. If you do not plan ahead, you may not get into the restaurant you want and could find that the only availabilities are at more expensive restaurants.

> *Note:* Advance reservations (formerly called priority seating) simply put you at the top of the list; it does not guarantee you a spot at a table when you arrive.

You can reserve as far as 90 days in advance for almost all WDW restaurants and mealtime events, including Character Meals. But if you want to see the *Hoop-Dee-Doo Musical Revue* (a dinner show) or attend Mickey's Backyard BBQ, plan to reserve much earlier. Reservations open two years in advance for *Hoop-Dee-Doo* and a year in advance for Mickey's BBQ. Call 407-WDW-DINE, or toll-free 800-828-0228, for all advance reservations.

• **Call from the parks for possible last-minute reservations.** If your plans change during your day at the park and you decide that you want to try a certain restaurant, or see if you can squeeze in a Character Meal, don't hesitate to call Dining Services from the park. You can make reservations anytime if there is availability. It never hurts to try.

You can call reservations toll free from any pay phone in Disney World. Simply dial *88; you won't have to deposit any coins. Or call 407-WDW-DINE from your cell phone if you have a nation-wide cell phone plan.

Tip: Program the reservations number into your cell phone so you always have it with you.

 Extra Food Tips from "Disney on a Dime"

Add in a grocery stop. As noted in *Chapter Two*, many taxis and limo services will allow a quick stop at a grocery store on your trip from the airport to your hotel. Look for and take advantage of this option. Being able to buy drinks, snacks, and possibly food for meals, is a great savings opportunity. Drinks in the parks are particularly expensive compared with the cost of bottled water and soft drinks in the grocery store.

Don't be shy or embarrassed about taking food into the parks. As we noted earlier, Disney does not publicly welcome outside food into the parks, but the underlying message is that it is OK.

Hydrate, hydrate, hydrate. We cannot stress enough the need to continually drink liquids while in the parks in order to stay hydrated. For the most part, you will be out in the elements of the sun and heat, and it is likely that you will be a lot more active than normal. It's said that people walk an average of five miles in a day at WDW.

Set a goal each day for how much you and your party need to drink to keep yourselves at a healthy level. Then be sure the children drink their water. Children are often so excited and caught up in all there is to see and do that they do not drink enough. This could be OK for a day, but after a couple of days they could start showing signs of dehydration, such as dry mouth, dizziness, and a reluctance to drink. If you see such signs in your children or other members of your party, or feel them yourself, it is important to take a long break. Relax and get some liquids into you. If the symptoms don't start going away after a few minutes, take the afternoon off or consult a nurse at one of the First Aid stations in the park.

> *Note:* Doctors say you can start feeling symptoms after as little as two hours of not drinking. Signs of more extreme dehydration include sunken eyes, the inability to pass urine or cry tears, lethargy, confusion, cold hands and feet, a rapid, weak pulse, rapid breathing, and high fever. Do not take this issue lightly. You could end up with a child in the hospital.

Check park closing time before finalizing your dinner plans. If you are visiting a park with an early closing (Animal Kingdom closes as early as 5 p.m. in some seasons), don't plan on eating dinner in the park. Eat offsite or in one of the other parks.

Don't waste money on big breakfasts. Unless your family is accustomed to eating a "hot" breakfast every single morning, don't waste money breakfasting at a restaurant — sit-down or counter-service. Try to eat what your family normally eats at home. If all everyone eats is cereal, then this should be fine for your vacation also.

Don't order food the kids won't eat. If the only thing the kids want is a handful of crackers and a juice box, let them have that while the adults eat something substantial. We have left all too many tables full of uneaten food we ordered for our children. To avoid wasting money and food, assess your children's needs before you order. If they aren't very hungry, or typically don't eat a whole lot, don't order for them.

Of course, you'll want to be sure they are eating enough. But that might well be a few bites of your meal or food you brought into the park with you.

Let kids share meals. Don't order one child's meal per child if your children are small or tend to be light eaters. A WDW child's meal is geared more towards a ten-year-old's appetite than a three-year-old's. If you have three small children, order two child's meals and split them among the three.

The "extra bun" trick. At the Electric Umbrella, in Epcot, you can order a double cheeseburger and fries for $7.19. Ask for an extra bun for the extra cost of only 70 cents. Take the extra patty off your double hamburger and voila, you have two cheeseburgers for an extra 70 cents. You'll have plenty of fixings for each burger because this quick-service restaurant has a toppings bar that is packed full of all of your favorite toppings and extras like mushrooms and peppers. You may feel odd doing this, but be assured that no one will notice or care.

> *$$aver Tip:* If you want to go to an even more extreme level, make your own sandwiches. Bring in meat and cheese in your cooler, order buns at the counter, and use the condiments at the toppings bar to provide the finishing touches. This could be a better option than preparing the sandwiches in your hotel and then fighting to keep them dry and unflattened by lunchtime.

> *Note:* These options will also work at Ray's Starlight Café and Pecos Bills, both in the Magic Kingdom.

Appetizers can be meals. When dining at a sit-down restaurant, the appetizers on the menu are often sufficient for a meal. If you do not wish to pay $17.99 for a Mogambo Shrimp Platter at the Rainforest Café, for example, you can buy the Tsunami Shrimp Cocktail for $9.99 instead. This is a good way to "treat" yourself on your vacation and avoid overeating at the same time.

If you feel that won't be quite enough, buy three appetizers and split them between two people. This way you can also try several different things. Or split an entrée between you; the portions are large. Note, though, that some restaurants will charge you a few dollars for splitting an entrée.

Leftovers. Most restaurants serve large portions and will happily pack up any leftovers for you to take back to your room. If you have a fridge and a microwave in your room, this can mean a "free" meal later in your stay.

More snack tips:

Buy in bulk and make your own " packs." Instead of buying individual pre-packaged bags of chips, crackers, and cookies, buy the regular size and pre-package them yourself using small plastic bags.

Make your own trail mix. Buy different bags of your favorite pretzels, nuts, etc… and mix them yourself.

Bring tubes of yogurt. Some things need to be pre-packaged, like yogurt (Gogurt®). Yogurt tubes are very convenient in the park and make a quick refreshing treat for everyone. If you have a freezer, in your hotel room, freeze them overnight. They will stay colder longer in the parks, and they can be eaten frozen for an extra cold treat.

Pack tubes of peanut butter. If your children love peanut butter, this can be a great energizing snack.

Note: The snacks are mainly for the kids, but don't forget to pack some extra ones for the adults.

Sign up for a Character Sundae — if available. If your kids are dying for a Character Meal (expensive at $9 to $13 per child and $17 to $28 per adult), you may be able to treat them to a Character Sundae instead. In the past, the Garden Grill Restaurant in Epcot's Land Pavilion had an afternoon Ice Cream Social with Characters that cost just $6.99 per person and gave you all the Character attention you would get at a Character Meal. The sundaes were delicious and the children got a free souvenir cup to take home. Disney even offered a complimentary scoop of ice cream with sprinkles to kids ages two and under.

Unfortunately, Disney stopped offering the Character Sundae when The Land pavilion was closed for the construction of its *Soarin'* attraction, which opened in 2005. It hasn't been reinstated as we go to press, but there is hope because it was popular with guests. If it appeals to you, we suggest calling 407-WDW-DINE a few weeks ahead of your visit to see if the Character Sundae is back on. If so, make a reservation for it.

> *Note:* This was an especially good deal because typically children are too excited to eat much at a Character Meal. If they don't consume the whole sundae, it isn't as much of a loss as it would be if you were paying for a full meal.

Get Animal Kingdom meal vouchers — if available. The Tusker House and Restaurantosaurus in Disney's Animal Kingdom may offer meal vouchers that could really save you money throughout the day. The vouchers, available on past visits but unavailable as we go to press, cost $6.38 for a child and $12.77 for an adult, including tax. The adult voucher offered some savings, while the child voucher was a truly great deal that offered really big savings. Both included a meal with a beverage plus an additional bottled water or soda and a snack (either an ice cream or popcorn). Best of all, you did not have to eat the meal where you bought the voucher. The meal part of the voucher could be redeemed at any counter-service restaurant in Animal Kingdom, and you could use the soda/bottled water and ice cream/popcorn vouchers at any kiosk or cart that sold those items. The potential savings were significant. Purchased separately, a child's meal cost $3.72 to $4.25 with tax; a water or soda, $2.66 to $3.20; an ice cream, $2.66 to $3.73, and a popcorn $2.66. If you bought everything on the high-end with cash, the total cost would be $10.96. So you saved $4.58 by buying a voucher. The adult meal voucher was also a good deal. While you wouldn't save $4.58, you would save a couple of dollars or more depending on what you ordered.

> *$$aver Tip:* If you used a child voucher for a Happy Meal at the McDonald's inside Restaurantosaurus, you also got a free Animal Kingdom toy, which made a nice souvenir.

Since Disney often withdraws and then reinstates special offers, we include the following tips to help you take best advantage of these special Animal Kingdom "meal plus certificates" if they are available when you visit:

The great thing about the vouchers, besides the savings, was the fact that you could use them throughout the day. Grab a soda around 10 a.m., eat lunch at 1:00 p.m., and then get an ice cream in time for the parade in the afternoon. Or interchange the vouchers for ice cream and soda. The price for a water/soda and an ice cream bar are pretty much the same, so vendors allowed you to get an ice cream bar with a soda certificate and vice versa. If you brought your own drinks to the park, you could use the drink certificate for ice cream instead.

While the vouchers were supposed to be good only on the day of purchase, we asked several vendors about it and they all said that there was no way they could know when meal certificates were purchased because there was no date printed on the vouchers and the colors did not change from day to day. So if you weren't hungry for a snack the day you bought the vouchers and you planned on coming back to Animal Kingdom during your trip, you could save your drink and ice cream certificates for your return visit.

This could all change, of course, if and when Disney reinstates the program. So be sure to check for an expiration date before using this tactic.

> *$$aver Tip:* Child vouchers could be used to feed adults, too. Just be warned that if you choose this option, there isn't a great selection of children's meals in Animal Kingdom. You will be limited to PB&J, macaroni and cheese, mini hotdogs, or chicken nuggets at McDonald's. The bonus came later in the day when you got that extra drink and ice cream.

The Disney Dining Experience Card

Eating at WDW's table-service restaurants and Character Meals can cost a small fortune. With the Disney Dining Experience Card, Annual Passholders and Florida residents can save 20% at many establishments, including the resort counter-service restaurants. The card, which costs $75 a year ($50 for Annual Passholders), covers the holder and up to nine other guests and applies to all food and beverages purchased at participating restaurants. Cards are not transferable, and the cardholder must present a driver's license or other photo ID when using the card.

If you plan to eat many meals out or are going to Disney World with a family or group, this could save you some serious money on meals. Say you are staying at a Value Resort and plan on eating most meals at its counter-service restaurant. Counter service at the Value Resorts is fairly economical and the card can make it even more so. Annual Passholders only have to spend $250 on meals to recoup the cost of a Dining card. This could be beneficial to families or groups that plan to make multiple trips throughout the year.

> *Note:* If you buy a Dining card to use mainly at counter-service restaurants, remember that the card is only good at the resort counter-service establishments (at least that's the case as we go to press). Thus, you will want to plan to go back to your resort (or any other WDW resort you fancy) for meals instead of eating them in the parks.

Benefits of the Dining card include:

• 20% off on all food and drinks at over 70 resort hotel and park restaurants.

> *Caution:* Discounts may be suspended at holidays; inquire when you make reservations or before you order.

• Valid for the cardholder and up to nine other people.

• FREE short-term (around 3 hours) resort and theme park parking for dining purposes. Parking must be paid for in advance, but after your meal you can take your receipt to Guest Services and get a full refund.

> *Note:* Annual Passholders get free theme-park parking at all times anyway.

• A FREE second membership for someone in your household. This can come in handy if you plan to split up at times during your trip. For example, if your spouse decides to go back to the hotel to swim and eat at the resort's food court, he/she can use one card while you use the other.

• 50% off admission to Pleasure Island and other discounts on entertainment.

• A newsletter to keep you informed of any changes in benefits or participating restaurants.

> *Caution:* This is also not a last-minute purchase. The only way you can get the card as we go to press is to call 407-566-5858. You cannot buy it online or at the parks. Allow four to six weeks for your card to arrive by mail.

Participating Restaurants

As we go to press, these restaurants, food courts, and lounges accept Disney's Dining Experience card. Double-check if you are interested in using it at a particular restaurant; the list can change at any time.

At the Resorts

All-Star Movies Resort: World Premiere Food Court

All-Star Music Resort: Intermission Food Court

All-Star Sports Resort: End Zone Food Court

Animal Kingdom Lodge: Boma, Jiko, Victoria Falls

Beach Club Resort: Beaches & Cream Soda Shop (excludes take-out shop), Cape May Cafe, Martha's Vineyard Lounge, Rip Tide Lounge

BoardWalk: ESPN Club, Flying Fish Cafe, Spoodles, Bellevue Lounge

Bonnet Creek Golf Club: Sand Trap Bar & Grill

Caribbean Beach Resort: Shutters at Old Port Royale

Contemporary Resort: California Grill, Chef Mickey's, Concourse Steakhouse, Outer Rim Lounge

Coronado Springs Resort: Maya Grill

Fort Wilderness Resort & Campground: Hoop-Dee-Doo Musical Revue (9:30 p.m. show only), Trail's End Restaurant

Grand Floridian Resort & Spa: 1900 Park Fare, Citricos, Garden View Lounge, Grand Floridian Cafe, Mizner's Lounge, Narcoossee's, Victoria & Albert's (excludes Chef's Table)

Old Key West Resort: Olivia's Cafe

Polynesian Resort: Kona Cafe, 'Ohana, Tambu Lounge, *Disney's Spirit of Aloha Show* (late show only)

Pop Century Resort: Everything Pop Food Court

Port Orleans Resort–French Quarter: Sassagoula Floatworks and Food Factory, Scat Cat's Club

Port Orleans Resort–Riverside: Boatwright's Dining Hall, River Roost

Saratoga Springs Resort: The Artist's Palette, The Turf Club

Wide World of Sports™: Official All-Star Cafe

Wilderness Lodge: Artist Point, Territory Lounge, Whispering Canyon Cafe

Yacht Club Resort: Yacht Club Galley, Ale and Compass Lounge, Yachtsman Steakhouse, Crews Cup Lounge

In Downtown Disney

Marketplace: Cap'n Jack's Restaurant

West Side: Wolfgang Puck Cafe, Planet Hollywood

In the Theme Parks

Epcot: Alfredo di Roma, Chefs de France, Nine Dragons, San Angel Inn, Bistro de Paris, Le Cellier Steakhouse, Biergarten Restaurant, Restaurant Marrakesh, Restaurant Akershus, Rose & Crown Pub & Dining Room, The Garden Grill, Coral Reef Restaurant

Disney-MGM Studios: Hollywood & Vine, 50's Prime Time Cafe, Tune-In Lounge, Mama Melrose's Ristorante Italiano, Sci-Fi Dine-In Theater Restaurant, The Hollywood Brown Derby

Magic Kingdom: The Crystal Palace, Cinderella's Royal Table, Liberty Tree Tavern, The Plaza Restaurant, Tony's Town Square Restaurant

Disney's Animal Kingdom: Tusker House Restaurant, Pizzafari, Flame Tree Barbeque, Restaurantosaurus

Entertainment and Dancing

Pleasure Island: Half-price admission for each Club Member, except for specially priced events.

Atlantic Dance Hall: FREE admission for members and their guests.

SAVE ON TICKETS

Disney offers a diverse menu of ticket options for WDW. Its "base ticket" admits you to one theme park per day, period. But you can add a number of options to tailor your tickets to your needs: the Park Hopper Option lets you move from park to park with the same base ticket; the Magic Plus Option admits you to some or all of WDW's water parks and entertainment areas; the No Expiration Option lets you keep any unused days (and options) on your ticket to use at any time in the future. Or you can opt for an Annual Pass or a Premium Annual Pass instead of a base ticket with or without options.

If much of this sounds unfamiliar, it may be because the current "Magic Your Way" ticket program has been in effect only since January 2, 2005. This system is a huge breakthrough for the budget-minded consumer. If the pre-2005 ticket prices discouraged you from planning a Disney World vacation, take a good look at the current pricing. A family of four (two adults and two children) can now go to Disney World for seven days for $530 less than it would have cost them before the "Magic Your Way" program went into effect. This savings alone could pay for your hotel room.

How Disney's Ticket Program Works

In essence, the current system gives you the freedom to construct a customized ticket for your specific needs. You only pay for the options you want. If all you want to do is go to one park per day, you can save a lot of money compared with the old pricing. And if you want to do it all, you can do that, too. With Magic Your Way, you can weigh the cost of each option against its value to you.

Base Tickets

Magic Your Way, allows guests to buy a base ticket in increments of one to ten days. The more days you buy, the cheaper the days get: for example, a one-day adult ticket costs $59.75 before tax while a 10-day base ticket costs just $208 ($20.80 per day).

> *Note:* If you're comparing, that's about the same as the old four-day Park Hopper pass cost.

Unless you purchase other options, each "day" on your base ticket admits you to one theme park, and only one. If you want to visit two parks on the same day, you will have to buy a Park Hopper® option (see below). Base tickets will not get you into the water parks or DisneyQuest (you will need a Magic Plus Pack option for that), and they expire 14 days after first use even if you haven't used up all your days.

> *$$aver Tip:* The Base Ticket is a great option for those who do not care about doing anything other than going to the four main theme parks. There's so much to see in the theme parks that this is the only ticket most people will need.

Park Hopper® option

If you aren't a one-park-a-day type of person, you may want to consider adding a park hopper option to your base ticket. The cost is a flat $35 per ticket, whether your base ticket is good for one day or ten. This option lets you move from park to park on the same day while using only one day on your base ticket. If you show up at the Magic Kingdom and it is extremely crowded, you can jump on the monorail and pop into Epcot, which is a lot roomier. Or you could go to Animal Kingdom for most of the day, move on to Disney-MGM Studios and catch the *Fantasmic!* show when Animal Kingdom closes (usually at 5:00 or 6:00 p.m.), and then end your day at Epcot's *Illuminations* fireworks show. If you are a resort guest, you could also use the hopper option to take maximum advantage of your Extra Magic Hours privileges (see *Chapter Five*) by visiting both the park designated for early entry and the park designated for extra evening hours on the same day.

> *$$aver Tip:* The park hopper option is not a necessity, but it can be a good investment. Say you can spend only two days at WDW, but want to see all four theme parks. Buying a two-day base ticket with a hopper option would let you do that for a good deal less than buying a four-day base ticket and give you more flexibility

as well. The option could also work for longer stays. If you buy a 10-day ticket, the incremental cost is only $3.50 a day. For that $3.50 extra, you'd gain a lot of flexibility. However, each guest has different needs and goals. You will have to evaluate whether the extra flexibility is worth the extra cost to you.

Magic Plus Pack option

The Magic Plus option extends your admission privileges to include some or all of the following: Disney's Typhoon Lagoon and Blizzard Beach water parks, Pleasure Island (Disney's nighttime entertainment area), Disney's Wild World of Sports complex, and DisneyQuest (an indoor interactive playground). You pay a flat rate of $45 per base ticket regardless of how many days your ticket covers. The number of extra admissions you get depends on the number of days on your ticket (see *Table*, below).

If you don't have the time or desire to go to the water parks or to the nighttime entertainment, this option is not for you. Our advice to those who have never been to Disney World and who do not plan on being there for more a week: Don't use this option because you may not have time to take full advantage of it. The WDW theme parks are so big and there are so many things to do in them that you probably won't have the time or energy to experience any of the "extra" parks and activities. But if your family can do a lot in a day or if you think you would like to spend a day or two in the water parks, buying this option could be an excellent use of your money.

> *Note:* Families with very small children may prefer their hotel swimming pool to a huge water park, especially if they are staying in one of the WDW resorts; all of them have very nice pools (see *Chapter Eight*).

Again, you will have to evaluate your own situation to determine whether the value is worth the price. If you decide to purchase the Magic Plus option, check the "extra tips" at the end of this chapter for ways to maximize its benefits.

No Expiration option

Under WDW's old ticketing system, any unused days on a ticket were good forever — and still are. But while an unused E ticket from 30 years ago is still valid today, Magic Your Way tickets expire 14 days after their first use — unless you purchase a No Expiration option for a nominal fee. The fee depends on the number of days on your base ticket (see *Table*, below).

Why would you want to consider this option? It could be a good investment. Say you only want to visit the parks for five days on this trip, but think you may want to come back in the future. A ten-day base ticket costs only $15 more than a five-day ticket. Thus, an adult can buy five extra days plus the no-expiration option for a 10-day pass for an extra $115. That is significantly less than the price of two separate five-day tickets at today's prices, and tomorrow's prices will almost certainly be higher. Taking advantage of your extra days will, of course, require a future trip, with all the expenses that entails.

Obviously, the no-expiration option is not for everyone. If you can afford only one trip to Disney World in the foreseeable future, don't get it. You won't be able to give or sell the unused days to anyone else.

You Can't Share Tickets and Passes

Disney's position is that tickets and Annual Passes are nontransferable and sharing invalidates them. Thanks to modern technology, Disney can and will enforce that policy on adult tickets and passes. Adults have to sign their tickets, and when they are first used, have their fingers scanned. The scanners measure and identify unique features of the guest's first two fingers and then record them onto the ticket. The user's fingers are scanned again on every subsequent use. If the scans don't match, the ticket is invalidated.

That's a change from the days before Magic Your Way tickets, when Disney monitored Annual Pass usage closely, but had no way to verify who was using its regular tickets. As a result, leftover days on a ticket could be shared with someone else or sold to local vendors or on eBay. In fact, you'll still find older tickets for sale in those venues (see below). The signature, which Disney maintains is required to protect guests in the event that their tickets are lost or stolen, also helps to prevent ticket sharing.

> *Note:* Children under the age of ten do not have to sign their tickets or have their fingers scanned, which some see as an invitation to save money by sharing children's tickets with friends. Bear in mind that Disney considers all tickets nontransferable.

Ticket and Option Pricing

Base ticket prices are based on age. An "Adult" is anyone age 10 or older; a "Child" is anyone between (and including) the ages of three and nine. Options cost the same for all. There are no discounts for seniors or for the disabled. Children under age three get in free.

The Table below is up-to-date as we go to press. Please check with Disney World before your trip to get the latest information. Disney changes the pricing of its tickets, Annual Passes, and options almost every year.

Ticket and Option Prices

# of Days	Adult (10+ yrs) Cost	Child (3-9 yrs) Cost	Park Hopper Option	Magic Plus Option	# Extra Magic Passes	No Expiration Option
1	$59.75	$48.00	$35.00	$45.00	2 Passes	None
2	$119.00	$96.00	$35.00	$45.00	2 Passes	$10.00
3	$171.00	$137.00	$35.00	$45.00	2 Passes	$10.00
4	$185.00	$148.00	$35.00	$45.00	3 Passes	$15.00
5	$193.00	$155.00	$35.00	$45.00	3 Passes	$35.00
6	$196.00	$157.00	$35.00	$45.00	4 Passes	$45.00
7	$199.00	$160.00	$35.00	$45.00	5 Passes	$55.00
8	$202.00	$162.00	$35.00	$45.00	5 Passes	$100.00
9	$205.00	$164.00	$35.00	$45.00	5 Passes	$100.00
10	$208.00	$167.00	$35.00	$45.00	5 Passes	$100.00

Annual Passes

An Annual Pass admits guests to all four WDW theme parks (Magic Kingdom, Epcot, Disney-MGM Studios, and Disney's Animal Kingdom) for 366 days (yes, you get an extra day for free). Unlike annual passes that you find at many amusement parks, which are good for a season or a calendar year, the WDW Annual Pass is good for 366 days from your first visit. You decide when your year starts and ends.

It is very important to understand this concept and use it to your advantage. By creating your own Disney Year, you can go to Disney World two years in a row on the same Annual Pass. For example, you could go in July of one year and June of the following year. That lets you stretch your money and put a big chunk of the cost of two vacations on the same tab, because the biggest expense of a WDW vacation is the cost of admission. By paying a little more up front for an Annual Pass, you and your family can go back for a second vacation at a fraction of the cost.

Annual Passes come in two flavors, regular and premium. The only difference between them (other than price) is that the Premium Annual Pass admits you to the water parks, Pleasure Island, DisneyQuest, and Disney's Wide World of Sports® Complex as well as to the theme parks.

Annual Pass privileges

• **Admission to the parks** for 366 days (plus the areas above for Premium Passholders). Annual passes expire on the day of their one-year anniversary (for example, January 1, 2008, if you first used it on January 1, 2007), giving you a year and a day of use.

• **Flexibility to move from park to park** at will. You can come and go at the theme parks without spending or wasting "days" There is a big difference emotionally, and ultimately physically, between having unlimited days and time in the parks (or on vacation in general) and counting the "days" that you have paid for and that you are either wasting or are not using to their ultimate value. With a regular ticket, you are charged a day at the park if you are there twelve hours or one. Once you walk into a park, you have "spent" that day and it is gone. With an Annual Pass you can focus on enjoying your vacation and not be consumed with counting days. If you want to sit around the pool all day and then go to a theme park to enjoy fireworks at night, an Annual Pass lets you do that without "losing" a day on your ticket.

• **Free parking at all the parks.** Unless you are an Annual Passholder or a resort guest, you will pay $8 a day to park at the theme parks. If you go to Disney World for a week, an Annual Pass will save you $56 on parking alone. You'll also save a bit of time and hassle because you won't have to pay every time you park; just show your Pass to the parking attendant.

• **Free Disney transportation** between the parks. (If you aren't a Passholder, you must be a WDW resort guest to have this privilege.)

• **Free quarterly newsletter.** You will be among the first to know of new developments. You will get a quarterly newsletter that outlines any new things that are happening in the parks and informs you of any new benefits being offered to Annual Passholders.

• **Discounts on merchandise and dining.** Passholders receive many discounts in the parks and at Downtown Disney stores and eateries. (The list changes often; check www.disneyonadime.com for an updated list of benefits.) You can also buy the Disney Dining Experience Card, which can save you 20% on dining at dozens of WDW restaurants (see *Chapter Three* for details).

• **Invitations to special events.** You'll be invited to special events. Typically when a new ride is opening, Disney offers a sneak peak to Annual Passholders. This is a great opportunity to be one of the first to try out new rides and view new attractions.

• **Periodic discounts on resort lodging.** Disney offers lodging specials for Passholders at various times throughout the year. They are a nice plus when available.

Annual Pass Pricing*		
Pass	**Adult** (Age 10+)	**Child** (Ages 3-9)
Regular Annual Pass	$395	$336
Premium Annual Pass	$515	$438
*Before tax		

Buying Tickets and Passes

You can purchase base tickets, options, and Annual Passes over the phone, online, or at the gate. You can also purchase base tickets and options (but not Annual Passes) at any Disney Store outside of Florida. By buying your tickets (or Annual Passes) in advance, you'll put a good chunk of your vacation expenses behind you before you leave for vacation. You may also save a long wait in the ticket line at the park gate. Best of all if you are buying tickets, as opposed to Annual Passes, you can save money by buying ahead. (There are no discounts for advance purchases of Annual Passes.)

To get a discount on Magic Your Way tickets, you must:

> • buy them online or at a Disney Store,
> • purchase a base ticket for five days or longer, and
> • add either a Park Hopper or Magic Plus option (or both) to your tickets.

The savings can be from $7 to $11 per ticket.

> *Caution:* You will have to pay shipping and handling fees if you buy online and want your tickets shipped to you. To avoid the fees, opt to pick up your tickets at a park Will Call window instead of having them mailed. Then bring your receipts and a valid photo ID to exchange your receipts for actual tickets or Annual Passes.

> *$$aver Tip:* Save time, and nerves, by picking up your tickets the day you arrive instead of waiting in line for them the next morning when you are anxious to start enjoying your day in the theme parks.

10-Day Ticket or Annual Pass: Which Should You Get?

If you plan to spend more than 10 days at WDW within a 12-month period, this is a no-brainer. Get the Annual Pass. The incremental cost is under $100 if you spend 11 or 12 days in the parks during your pass year (compared with the cost of buying a 10-day ticket with a Hopper option plus a one-day or two-day ticket without a Hopper), and you come out ahead financially if you spend 13 or more days — and that's without factoring in the discounts and the free parking the pass gives you.

If 10 days is your limit, the choice is more difficult. Here are some factors to consider:

• **Will you stay for a long time only once?** Or do you plan to visit at least twice? If you plan to stay for one 10-day stretch and don't plan to return in the foreseeable future, a 10-day ticket with a Hopper option will save you $152 compared with the cost of an Annual Pass. If, however, you plan to visit at least twice in the foreseeable future, you'll have to add a No Expiration option to your ticket, bringing your savings down to a mere $52 compared with the cost of an Annual Pass.

• **When will you be back?** If you plan to visit at least twice, do you want to come back in less than a year? Or would you prefer to come back later? The biggest potential benefit of having a 10-day ticket with no expiration option rather than an Annual Pass is that you can save on two Disney World vacations without taking both of them within a 12-month period. You could take one now and the next 10 years later.

• **Can you take advantage of the discounts and parking benefits?** You don't need free parking if you are staying onsite; it comes with your lodging. Also, if your goal is to spend as little as possible during your visit(s), you may not be doing enough dining and shopping to save the difference in price between the pass and the 10-day ticket through Annual Pass discounts. Chances are, though, if you are considering either option, your vacation budget is large enough to allow some discretionary spending. If you manage to nail a good deal on a resort room through a Passholder discount, you might more than recoup the difference in price on that alone.

Extra Ticket Tips from "Disney on a Dime"

Buy an Annual Pass if at all possible. It will let you visit more often, because your admissions are already paid for. Long weekends at WDW could be affordable if you live close enough, and if you live farther away, you can plan a couple of major vacations during the life of your Pass. As we note above, by taking two vacations on the same Annual Pass, you can cut the total cost of your second vacation by half or more.

Buy your tickets over time, as you save up the money for them, instead of buying them all at once. We suggested this in *Chapter One*, but it bears repeating. It is easier to plan and pay for the rest of your vacation when you have your ticket purchases out of the way. Buying them one at a time can make the cost a little easier for your vacation budget to swallow.

Keep your ticket receipts. Be sure to keep your receipts and your tickets or ticket vouchers in separate areas (before and during your trip). Make copies of each (front and back) as this can help verify your purchase if you should lose your voucher or tickets and need to replace them.

Visit WDW before your child turns three. Remember the phrase, "Before Three, They're Free!!" Disney only charges admission to guests age three and older. If you have a child who is going to turn three around the time of your planned vacation, you may want to adjust the dates so that you go right before you would have to pay. A few weeks' difference can make a big difference money-wise.

Note: For those who think an almost three-year old will not enjoy or remember Disney World, think again. In our experience, this is a "magical" time to take a little one. Our eighteen-month old could name the different parks and the rides in the different lands after one of our trips. The little ones can have a blast, too.

Don't buy one-day tickets. A trip to Disney World is too big an investment for a single day in a single theme park. You could add a park hopper option to make a whirlwind visit to all four parks, but it would add almost 60% to the cost of your ticket. Besides, even a Disney veteran would have a tough time seeing all that even one park has to offer in a single day.

If you're dying to see Disney World and a one-day ticket is all you can afford, rethink your vacation priorities. You'll have to pay for transportation to get to WDW and quite possibly for lodging as well. (Since you have to eat anyway, we won't count food costs.) Don't spend your time and several hundred dollars to get to Disney World and then waste them by staying only a single day. Save up until you have enough set aside to cover a longer stay. (*Chapter One* offers many strategies for building your vacation budget.)

Exception: If you are in the area on business, or just passing through town, and you want to pop in and see Mickey, buying a one-day ticket is the cheapest — in fact, the only — option. One day is better than none.

Take advantage of the "extra days" offered by the Magic Plus option. When you add Magic Plus options to your base ticket, you are actually buying extra days of activity. You'll get more for your money if you spread these days out over your stay, spending full days in the theme parks and using your Magic Plus "extra days" as breathers. For example, say you are staying seven days. Buying a five-day ticket with the Magic Plus option would let you go to the parks for two days, and then relax on the third: sleep late, spend part of the day in a water park and the rest just taking in the resorts and grounds outside of the parks. Go back to the theme parks on days four and five, then repeat your "day off" plan — maybe this time spending part of the day in Downtown Disney, where two of your Magic Plus options will admit you to DisneyQuest and to Disney's Wide World of Sports. Finish your vacation with a bang, by hitting the highlights of your favorite theme park again on your last day.

Remember, the number of Magic Plus options you get depends on the length of your base ticket. You can have three days of Disney fun on a one-day ticket with Magic Plus and fifteen days on a ten-day ticket. Just be aware that your number of days in the four major theme parks is limited to the actual number of days on your base ticket (one and ten in the examples above).

Beware buying tickets on eBay. Most of the tickets sold on eBay are the used Park Hopper passes with (so the seller claims) unused days with no expiration date. Not only is there no way to verify how many days are left on these passes until you arrive at Disney World, but also the savings are generally small to nonexistent. Single-day tickets typically sell for more on eBay than Disney charges at the gate.

Beware local ticket vendors. If you drive around the area just outside of WDW, you are bound to see dozens of places that claim they have Disney tickets for 50% off or even cheaper. Buyer beware when dealing with these establishments. Typically these vendors sell partially used passes. There is no way to verify that there are valid days left on the passes and no money-back guarantees if you get caught short. Disney will not help you if you buy passes from unauthorized dealers.

Get free tickets (if you have the time and patience). If you don't mind sitting through 90 minutes of sales pitches, there are numerous timeshare developments in the Orlando area that offer free one-day passes for your time.

Most of these presentations start around 6:30 or 7:00 in the morning and include a free breakfast. After their sales pitch, they'll give you your tickets and you can be on your way. The deal is typically one pass for every adult.

We knew one couple who used this technique and went to the parks for a whole week for free. Every morning they would get up early, eat the free breakfast, listen to a sales pitch, get their free tickets, and then head for the parks. If that works for you, look for ticket vendors in the Orlando area. You won't have any trouble finding them.

> *Caution:* It is OK to sign up for timeshare presentations through these guys, but do not buy tickets from them (see above).

Get discounted "Convention Tickets." Disney allows some hotels to offer discounted "Convention Tickets" to their guests. These typically expire within 10 days and cannot be upgraded with the "no expiration" option. They are only available through hotels and brokers. If you just need some quick tickets and do not intend to return, this could be a good deal.

Stay longer if you can. The low incremental cost of adding extra days to your ticket is well worth considering when planning your vacation. If it costs $1,000 to fly your family to Disney World, it is probably a good investment of $100 more in tickets to stay seven days instead of three or four, if you can afford the additional lodging costs.

For Adults, the difference in price between a:
- 3-day ticket and a 4-day ticket is only $14.
- 4-day ticket and a 5-day ticket is only $8.
- 5-day ticket and a 6-day ticket is only $3.
- 6-day ticket and a 7-day ticket is only $3.
- 7-day ticket and an 8-day ticket is only $3.
- 8-day ticket and a 9-day ticket is only $3.
- 9-day ticket and a 10-day ticket is only $3.

In most cases, the incremental cost is even less for Child tickets.

- Buy Them on Sale Before You Go

- Shop Wisely at Disney World

- Autographs & Scrapbooks

- Photos & Videos

- Other Low- & No-Cost Options

- Extra Tips

SAVE ON SOUVENIRS

No vacation is complete without souvenirs. Walt Disney World is filled with eye candy, much of it for sale. As each day goes by, the eyes of children (and adults!) grow big with the desire to take some of it home. Fortunately, there are many ways to save big bucks on souvenirs. With a little planning, you can come home with meaningful souvenirs of your big vacation without breaking the bank.

Buy Souvenirs at Sales Before You Go

This may sound odd, but it makes great financial sense. Shop the sales at the local Disney Stores and discount stores that carry Disney toys and clothing. Just as some people shop the sales and put away gifts for Christmas and birthday gifts, you can stash away Disney stuff to surprise the kids with or to give as souvenirs on your vacation. Several times a year, the Disney Store has huge 75%-off sales on practically everything in the store. Buy surprises for each of your children for every day of your vacation. They will be so excited about what their surprises are going to be, they won't pester you for anything! Things you can give them include:

- Disney toys
- Disney movies on DVD or video
- T-shirts adorned with favorite Disney characters
- Sunglasses
- Canteens decorated with Disney characters
- Dress-up items
- Disney coloring books

• Disney beach towels

Once, we bought a Disney World play set on clearance at a discount store for $5.00. While at Disney World, we saw the same exact play set in a gift shop for $28.00! Most of the time, you can find items at local discount stores and the Disney Store that are identical to or the same quality as those you will see at Disney World. The big difference is that they are much cheaper.

Get to know your local Disney Store managers. They will be extremely helpful in letting you know when to come in and what could be going on sale. They are a great resource for getting your special items at a magical price.

Shop Wisely at Disney World

While WDW generally charges more than you would pay for the same item at home, there is no shortage of reasonably priced items in its shops and stands if you keep your eyes open. In fact, many of the best souvenirs are free for the taking. You just have to be creative. Here are some ideas to get you started:

Start an Inexpensive Collection

Get your children to start a collection of reasonably priced items that will display well at home. The goal is to buy something meaningful that won't get lost in the mass of toys when you get home. Some examples of things kids and adults can collect:

• **Die cast collectible ride cars.** Collectible ride cars (about $6 each) are available in gift shops at ride exits as well as souvenir shops all around the parks. That means you can collect a car for nearly every ride, so you will want to pick and choose. If money is tight, have your children (or yourself) pick out their favorite ride of the entire trip and buy only the car for that ride. When you go back again to WDW, you can pick out another. This is a great collection to start and a great way to remember each trip.

• **Pressed pennies.** Pressed coins are a favorite among adult collectors and children, and at a cost of just 50 cents plus the penny, they are very affordable. There are many, many, many presses around WDW property offering a large variety of characters and themes. Go to the guest relations or lobby concierge desk at the parks and resorts to get a list of the penny press locations and start a "hunt" to find your favorite characters to press into your pennies. Display books to keep them in are available at most gift shops at Disney. Or simply glue them into a scrapbook.

Note: For a buck plus the quarter, you can also impress quarters.

• **Charm bracelets.** You'll find charm bracelet-making stations in WDW's major gift shops. Charm bracelets are fun for girls to start, and they can add a charm or two on each visit to Disney World. Charms run from about $3 to $30 or more. You'll find an abundance of the $3 variety. Charm necklaces are also available.

• **Disney pins.** Pin trading is a great tradition among Disney fans worldwide. Pins start at $8 apiece in the parks, however, which means that collecting them can get expensive fast. We suggest you go online to www.ebay.com and buy a mixed "lot" of Disney pins. Make sure they have the Disney trademark before you buy them and then display them on a lanyard that you can wear when you go to the parks. If your favorite character didn't come on any of the pins in the lot you bought, look for that character on a Cast Member's pin lanyard. When you spot it, trade one of your pins for the one you want. It is Disney policy that Cast Members must trade with you. You could turn the search into a "treasure hunt," with a prize of some kind for the family member who spots it first.

• **Character beanie dolls.** The shops at almost every ride exit sell character beanies dressed up in the costumes that suggest the ride — a "Roadie" Mickey Mouse complete with a backstage pass and bandana, for example, in the *Rock 'n' Rollercoaster* shop, Goofy dressed up as a bellhop for the *Tower of Terror* (both in Disney-MGM Studios), or Mickey in a racing uniform for Epcot's *Test Track*. The beanies are only $8 apiece and can be collected over time.

Autographs and Scrapbooks

It's fun to collect autographs and items to use in scrapbooks. Encourage your children in those activities while you are at Disney World. They'll come home with meaningful souvenirs that cost little to nothing.

Take Autograph Collecting to New Heights

Kids love to collect autographs of their favorite Characters. With a little imagination, you can help them do that and more. Be sure to bring a pen along

• **Buy or make autograph books.** There are great autograph books available at many of the Disney souvenir shops. At a cost of about $6, they are inexpensive and fun. Better yet, have the kids make their own autograph books at home, before your vacation, from a journal or other book filled with blank pages. You can buy these at a discount store for a dollar or two, and the kids can decorate them however they want. Children will often pull out their auto-graph books long after the vacation to look through them and admire the way each character signed their name, whether silly or fancy.

> *Tip:* Make this souvenir even more special by having the characters always sign on the same side of the book (left or right). Then use the facing page for pictures of your children standing next to the character whose signature is opposite. It makes a great scrapbook.

• **Let storybooks do double duty**. Bring along a favorite Disney storybook and ask the featured characters to sign it. You can buy a book expressly for this purpose or simply bring one from home that your child loves. When you see the characters from the story in the parks or during a character meal, have them sign the blank pages at the front or back. This makes a great keepsake.

• **Collect Cast Member autographs in Epcot's World Showcase**. Collecting character autographs is a common practice in all Disney theme parks, but few people think of getting autographs from Cast Members (employees). Almost all the Cast Members who work in the "countries" (country pavilions) in Epcot's World Showcase are natives of the country in which they work. In Mexico, for example, the Cast Members are from Mexico, in China from China, and so on.

For a really special autograph collection, get the signatures of a Cast Member from each country in World Showcase, and ask each one to write something in their native language. You could have a phrase like "Good Morning," "Hello," or "Happy Holidays" picked out, so you can see what that phrase would look like in each language.

The Cast Members are very cooperative. They enjoy talking about their home countries and are eager to share their native languages and cultures. On our last trip, several Cast Members in China helped with a school project our daughter was doing on their country. They wrote out several names and phrases that she was able to incorporate into her presentation.

Collect Items for a Souvenir Scrapbook

Many items that are free in the parks are awesome in scrapbooks. If you want to get fancier, you can buy packages of Disney-specific scrapbooking materi-als at gift shops (at home or in Orlando) to add to the items you pick up at Disney World. Hobby Lobby, Michaels, and other craft stores carry plenty of scrapbooking supplies at discounted prices. Be careful, though, because these things can get expensive. A little can go a long way when combined with all of the free things you can bring back from Disney World.

These WDW freebies make great souvenirs:

Tickets. The tickets you will get and use throughout your visit have a Disney character on them and make great souvenirs for your scrapbook.

Unused or extra FASTPASSes. When you use the FASTPASS system, you are issued a small ticket that has the name of the ride, the date, and the time it is good for. These are great souvenirs. They not only show the rides you rode and when you rode them, but also look good in a scrapbook because each ride's FASTPASS is a different color and is printed with a unique design.

Try to collect one for every FASTPASS ride. To build your collection either get FASTPASSes that you don't need to use because the line is short or you've already been on the ride, or put your park ticket into the FASTPASS machine twice, one right after another. The machine will issue one valid pass and one that is marked "Not a Valid FASTPASS" (because you are only allowed one FASTPASS within a given time period). Both will have the ride name, date, and time on them.

Napkins. Keep napkins from park restaurants and eateries. They have Mickey Mouse, the Walt Disney World logo, and the restaurant's name on them. Where else could you get these?

Park maps and parade schedules. Upon entry to a park (and at any park gift shop), you will find free, illustrated park maps and a separate Times Guide listing the schedule for the day's (or week's) shows and parades. These are free! Grab as many maps as you want or need. Put one in your scrapbook and hang the others up in the kids' rooms when you get home. Or just keep them where you can pull them out to remember the good times you had at the different places and rides.

Stickers. Throughout your stay, look for opportunities to get free stickers from Cast Members. When you see them standing outside a ride or on the sidewalk with a big role of stickers, ask for one or two. Most of these stickers have Mickey or Minnie and Walt Disney World on them, but others are unique. For example, we received stickers on the ferry to the Magic Kingdom that had a sailor Mickey on them. Save the special stickers in your scrapbook. Or stick them on your camcorder, camera or stroller and you will often be reminded of your great vacation.

Computer printouts and trivia prizes. At some of the Mr. Potato Head and My Little Pony play stations in the Once Upon a Toy store in Downtown Disney, there is a place to print things out. You can print out postcards of Mr. Potato Head or My Little Pony to take home. Or print out trivia questions. If you answer them right and take the sheet to a clerk, you'll get a small prize and a certificate.

Let Guidebooks Do Double Duty, Too

Buy your children their own guidebook for the trip (there are several aimed at children). They are full of color photos of the rides and come with spaces that let your kids write about their experiences. Use these guides before you go to help the kids understand where they are going and what they can do there. Use them while you are at Disney World so the kids can participate in the planning and document their days. Then, when you get home, use the guidebooks for scrapbooking. Let the kids cut out the pictures of the rides, characters, and other sites to put in their photo albums and scrapbooks. Be sure you take out any special pages where the kids documented their trip and incorporate them into a scrapbook.

Photos and Videos

WDW is packed with photo opportunities — special shows, spectacular scenery, your kids meeting characters, and family and friends enjoying themselves. Children love to reminisce long after the vacation by thumbing through all of the pictures and watching videos of themselves on vacation. Capture the magic on film and you'll have a wonderful souvenir.

Note: Some rides and attractions do not allow flash photography. Check the signs on your way in or listen for an announcement from a cast member.

• **Don't buy hats and props — just take your picture in them**. Numerous souvenirs that are funny and entertaining are things you would probably never use again. A great example of this: we saw an adult man walking around Epcot with a huge Nemo clown fish hat on his head. He would clearly never wear this outside of Walt Disney World — at least we don't think he would. Instead of buying items like these, simply put them on in the store and have someone in your party take your picture.

There are tons of hats and unique items available to use as props, so the options for this are virtually endless. Put on a huge sombrero in Mexico. In Norway, get your picture snapped wearing a Viking hat. Turn yourself into a fairy tale character in Magic Kingdom or an exotic mammal in Animal Kingdom.

On our last trip to WDW, we witnessed a group of guys outside the *Pirates of the Caribbean* ride. Instead of buying an eye patch, plastic sword, pirate's vest, and a pirate's hat, they all put these items on and had a group photo taken. They now have a photo that will spark a lifetime of memories and it didn't cost them a dime for the props.

> *Note:* Cast Members don't mind if you do this. Just don't open any sealed items and put everything back where you found it when you are done.

• **Get your picture taken by a professional for free.** When you enter the theme parks, look out for the Disney photographers. They walk up and down Main Street in the Magic Kingdom and in every opportune place in all of the parks. Let these individuals take your picture with their cameras and then ask them to take another picture with your camera.

This is much better than asking another tourist who happens to be standing by. You get a professional photo without paying a fee. The photographers don't mind taking the picture; they'll do it gladly.

• **Email yourself and others a personal photo.** In Epcot's *Mission: SPACE*, Innoventions, and the Kodak What If! Labs located at the exit of the *Journey Into Your Imagination* ride, you can take a digital picture of yourself or your group. Email a copy to your friends with a short message. And don't forget to email one to yourself to print and put into your photo album when you get home. What a great free souvenir!

Other Low- and No-Cost Souvenirs

There are plenty available. Just keep your eyes open and a hand on your wallet.

• **Send ahead for free autographed character photos.** Contact the Walt Disney Company before your trip to request autographed character photos for each of your children. Disney provides this service free to all who ask. Just send them a letter or postcard requesting a picture and autograph from your favorite character. Your only cost is the postage. You are allowed one picture per mailed request. Mail requests to:

The Walt Disney Company
Attn: Fan Mail Dept.
500 South Buena Vista Street
Burbank, CA 91521

If you want the pictures before your trip, so that you can give them to the kids during your trip, as souvenirs, mail your request(s) a couple of months before your trip and allow four to six weeks for the pictures to arrive.

• **Deck your head with Mouse Ears.** The classic Mickey Mouse Club mouse ears hat (about $6) still makes a great souvenir. If you go to The Chapeaux on Main Street in Magic Kingdom, they'll embroider your name on the back of it for free.

• **Check out Mr. and Mrs. Potato Head** — *Disney version.* At Once Upon a Toy in Downtown Disney and in some gift shops in the parks, you will find a huge Mr. Potato Head display with tons of Disney-exclusive parts, which are available only from Disney. If you want to get this unique toy, they will give you a box to fill with as many pieces of Mr. Potato Head as you can fit inside and charge you a flat rate per box ($18 as we go to press).

The most cost efficient way to get this cool guy and gal with all their Disney gear, is to purchase the classic Mr. and Mrs. Potato Head ahead of time at a discount store for about $5. Then when you visit WDW, just stuff the box you get with the Disney parts rather than taking up most of the space with the head. As long as you can close the top of the box, any number of parts you squeeze inside is OK. Little ones just love this!

> *Tip:* If you do buy the head in the parks, get as many parts as possible by filling the inside of the potato with parts as well as packing parts around it.

Some of the Potato Head displays include interactive screens where kids can play games and print out postcards with Mr. Potato Head to take home.

• **Look into My Little Pony** — **Disney version.** You'll find a My Little Pony display in the back of Once Upon a Toy. Kids can play with the ponies by dressing them up, adding accessories, and giving them a ride in their very own "Tea Cup." The setup is identical to the Mr. Potato Head display in the same store. Interactive screens in the area allow kids to play games and print things off. The cost of buying a pony and accessories is $18. Again, this includes anything you can fit into the box. Our recommendation is to forego getting a pony and just buy the accessories. You can get a My Little Pony anywhere, but the exclusive Disney accessories can only be purchased here. If you don't want to spend the $18, just take a picture of your personalized pony.

• **Enjoy craft-making at the Kidcot Fun Stops in Epcot.** EPCOT has a program that helps young children become engaged in the countries of World Showcase. In every country pavilion, there is a little station where the children can color a mask and get a special emblem and a stamp (all for free!). The crafts projects make great souvenirs and, if the kids collect stamps from every pavilion, they also get a prize. We won't spoil the surprise, but we will say that the last time we did this, it was something we could hang on the wall; it is a great souvenir that reminds the whole family of Epcot. Our children talk about their projects all the time and about how much fun they had visiting the countries. Before we participated in this program, our kids thought World Showcase was boring.

> *Note:* The Kidcot stops have proven so popular that Disney is adding them in Future World. On a recent trip, we found Kidcot stations in the Test Track and Living Seas pavilions. You'll probably find them in additional Future World pavilions when you visit.

• **Collect postcards.** These are among the cheapest souvenirs. You can buy them individually or in packets in the parks and resorts. If you're staying at a Disney resort, you may even be able to get some for free. Ask at the front desk if they have any complimentary postcards you can have. Use the postcards you get to as substitutes for photos you were either unable or not skilled enough to take yourself.

Extra Souvenir Tips from "Disney on a Dime"

Give the kids some autonomy in choosing souvenirs. In the weeks and months before your big trip, help each child build up a personal vacation fund. Your children will be more careful in their choices if they have their own money to spend, and souvenir shopping won't be such a burden on your vacation spending budget because the cost will already be taken care of, at least in part.

Give Disney Dollars for gifts and allowances. Disney dollars come in denominations of $1, $5, and $10 (plus $50 during the 18-month celebration of Disneyland's 50th anniversary, which runs through Fall 2006). They are decorated with Disney images and can be used like U.S. currency in the Disney parks, resorts, and cruise line, as well as in Disney Stores. They make great gifts for your children in the months leading up to the big vacation. Stuff their stockings with them. Give them for birthdays. Ask other relatives to give Disney Dollars for presents, and pay your children their allowance in full or part with them.

Disney Dollars can be purchased at any Disney Store on a dollar for dollar basis with no fees or sales tax added. You can also order by calling 407-566-4985 (press 2 for ticketing) or writing (see below). You can order up to $50 in Disney Dollars with a credit card, or up to $650 if you pay by check or money order (be sure to specify the denominations you want). There is $10 shipping fee and deliveries must be signed for since they contain cash equivalents.

> Walt Disney World Ticketing
> P.O. Box 10140
> Lake Buena Vista, FL 32830

You'll also find Disney Dollars on eBay.

Let kids earn vacation spending money. Have your children work and earn their vacation money throughout the year. Make up extra projects around the house for them to do or agree to dedicate part of their regular allowance towards their personal vacation fund. After they've earned their own spending money, they might spend it more wisely.

Once at WDW, give your kids a spending budget for each day in the parks — or help them set one for themselves. Let the kids know that when their spending budget is gone for the day, it is gone for good! Be diligent about this so you won't overspend your souvenir budget. They may choose to pool their money over a couple of days to buy something special that costs more.

Bring your own Disney hat and get it embroidered for free. The Chapeaux on Main Street in Magic Kingdom will embroider any hat made by Disney. You do not have to purchase it in the shop. You can buy mouse ears or other Disney headgear outside the park or bring hats from a previous trip. As long as it has Disney somewhere on it, Cast Members in the shop will embroider it for free.

Mail your kids a postcard from their favorite characters. For an extra special souvenir for the kids, have characters sign a postcard for each child and then mail them home before you leave. If you have them signed and mail them home on the first day of your visit, there's a chance that these personalized greetings will be waiting for your children when you get home.

Get yourself a Monorail Co-Pilot License. It is a little known fact that you can ride in the very front car of the monorail, along with the driver. This treat is available to everyone. Just ask the attendant if you can ride there. There is normally a special bench set aside at the front of the monorail with spots for four special riders. After your ride, you'll get a Monorail Co-Pilot License to commemorate your special trip. Put it in your scrapbook or hang it on the wall when you get home.

> *Note:* Only four guests may sit up front at a time, so large groups will have to split up.

Celebrate a child's birthday and get a free birthday button. If it is your birthday, you can go to Guest Relations and they will give you a free "It's My Birthday" button to wear. This is an extra special souvenir that commemorates your special day in the park.

> *Note:* It also can get you a lot of attention. While Disney World does not officially give Birthday Boys and Girls special treatment, Cast Members will call them out in a crowd, acknowledge their birthday, and sometimes even bring them a free dessert with their meal.

Collect free soft-drink cups. Most of the sit-down restaurants serve children their drinks in small plastic cups. These are similar to the drink cups you'll find at a Red Lobster or Bennigan's, with one big difference: the cups at WDW restaurants have Disney decorations.

> *$$aver Tip:* You do not have to buy a soft drink to get a cup. Water is free and it is also served in a Disney cup.

Snag free items from your resort room. If you are staying at a WDW resort, don't overlook the free resort stationery and pens in your room. Pack them away immediately: they might be restocked during your stay. Resort soaps, shampoos, and Do Not Disturb signs can also double as collector's items.

Get on "the list" at the Disney Store. Most Disney Stores have a list of valuable, frequent customers. Store managers use it to notify customers of special sales and opportunities. When they have a sale that offers discounts of 50% or more, they will call you and let you know about it. Recently we received a call offering us a special "Friends and Family" deal that entitled us to an additional 20% off every item in the store. Most items were already 50% off. The additional 20% discount we got meant that we could buy the item for 60% off its original price.

If you are lucky enough to live near a Disney Store (now owned by The Children's Place), get on their mailing list. Multiple times a year, they will mail

40%-off coupons to everyone on the list. These coupons are good for your entire purchase and apply to the price after any and all other discounts have been taken.

> *$$aver Tip:* The Disney Stores typically receive new pricing and sales information on Tuesday nights. The associates stay after hours and reduce the items scheduled for sale or clearance. So, Wednesdays are the best days to check out what just went on sale.

Take advantage of Annual Passholder discounts. Some of the shops in Downtown Disney and the parks extend a 10% discount to Annual Passholders, including World of Disney, the biggest store on WDW property (and the biggest Disney Store in the world). Among the others are:

> Planet Hollywood (also in Disney-MGM Studios)
> Virgin Megastore
> House of Blues Shop
> Rainforest Café shop (also in Disney's Animal Kingdom)
> Eurospain by Arribas Brothers

Participating stores change from time to time, so be sure to check: www.disneyonadime.com for an up-to-date list before your trip.

> *$$aver Tip:* Since World of Disney offers just about anything you will find in the big shops in the theme parks, which don't extend the discount, you can pick out the souvenirs you want to buy while you're in the parks and then make a trip to World of Disney to save a few bucks on them.

Consider selling duplicate souvenir items on eBay. With so many free souvenir items available in the parks (napkins, etc.), you could easily collect a few extras to share with folks who didn't think to pick them up when they were at Disney World, or who haven't yet made the trip. You won't make a lot, but every extra dollar can help to pay for your next WDW vacation.

SAVE ON LODGING

Part 1: Save While Staying Onsite

The biggest costs of your WDW vacation will be the price of admission and the price of your hotel. You can't do a whole lot about the price of admission, but you can make choices that will make a big difference in how much you pay for your hotel or other lodging, whether you stay onsite or off.

Staying in a Walt Disney World Resort hotel, or "on property," as the WDW folks say, is usually more expensive than staying offsite. You can't beat the magic, however, and there are some built-in transportation money-savers that can help make up for the higher room cost (see "Benefits," below).

In this chapter, we'll discuss the pros and cons of staying onsite, introduce WDW's resort categories, and offer a number of strategies for saving money on resort rooms and getting the best value for your money. In the following two chapters, we'll offer details on affordable WDW hotels (*Chapter Seven*) and then turn our attention to saving money by (and while) staying offsite (*Chapter Eight*).

Resort Benefits

The benefits of staying on property range from the atmosphere and guaranteed quality to special guest privileges such as early entry to the theme parks and being able to charge all your theme park purchases to your room, even popcorn.

Disney Magic 24/7

Going off property reminds you that there is a real world out there. That can sometimes detract from the experience. Some parts of the area surrounding WDW are very nice, but there are also a lot of places that aren't as clean and neat as Disney's World. By never leaving the property, children and adults alike can live the fairytale life throughout their visit. You will always be surrounded by Disney characters, signs, and buildings.

"Extra Magic Hours"

Most days of the week, Disney offers its resort guests either early entry into one of its theme parks (an hour before the general public) or the opportunity to stay in a designated park up to three hours after closing time. The early entry option is great for early risers (most families with small children). It lets you hop on your favorite rides before the lines grow longer. The extended evening hours are a great way to keep playing into the night.

Extra Magic Hours privileges are extended exclusively to guests of the WDW resorts, Shades of Green, and the Swan and Dolphin hotels in the Epcot area, and Hilton Resort at Downtown Disney.

> *Note:* While your resort key entitles you to Extra Magic Hours privileges, you will still need an Annual Pass or admission ticket to enter the parks. On any given day, the park designated for extended evening hours will be different from the park open for early entry. Therefore, if you want to take advantage of both the early and extended hours on the same day, you will need to add a Hopper option to your base ticket if you don't have an Annual Pass.

"Magical Express" service

At least through 2006, during its "Happiest Celebration on Earth" festivities (to celebrate Disneyland's 50th anniversary), Disney resort guests can take advantage of free round-trip shuttle service between Orlando International Airport and any of the WDW resort hotels (see *Chapter Two* for details).

Guaranteed quality

You are guaranteed clean, up-to-date facilities in any WDW resort hotel. Disney prides itself on its competent and skilled workers. Your room will always be professionally cleaned and prepared in a loving Disney way. Guests often share stories of times they have returned to their rooms and found their Disney dolls on the dresser positioned as in a scene out of a movie. This kind of attention to detail makes a Disney resort stay extra special. Offsite, standards of cleanliness and service vary drastically from hotel to hotel.

Free Disney transportation

The transportation system at Disney World is free to its resort guests and second to none. It includes buses, monorails, and ferries that connect to each other and run between the parks and the resorts, as well as from park to park. The buses that service the majority of resorts can get you to the theme parks, the Ticket and Transportation Center, Downtown Disney and WDW's two water parks in no time at all.

Free parking

Resort guests who prefer to drive can park free anywhere on Disney World property. Parking for outside guests is $8 a day, unless they have an Annual Pass. That's a savings of $56 a week for parking alone.

Close to everything

No matter where you stay on property, you can get to and from the theme parks and other Disney properties in a matter of minutes. That means you'll be able to go back to your hotel to rest or grab a bite without wasting a lot of time. When you have to leave Disney property, you need to add at least 10 minutes — and often a good deal more — to your round-trip, which could make resting or eating in your hotel room problematic.

> *Note:* If you're willing to get a second mortgage on the house, you can stay at the deluxe Polynesian, Contemporary, or Grand Floridian resorts and walk or monorail to Magic Kingdom in no time.

Room key charge privileges

Resort guests can use their room keys in place of cash or credit cards at all of the restaurants, gift shops, and popcorn stands in the theme parks, or anywhere on property. If it's for sale, you can buy it with your room key. You never have to worry about losing your wallet, cash, or credit cards. You can stash them in your free in-room safe.

> *Note:* If you lose your key, you'll only need to make one call to cancel it and get a replacement. No need to call five different companies and wait for new cards as you would if your wallet were lost.

Park purchases delivered free to your room

If you find that special snow globe or huge toy at the beginning of your day, you can buy it and have it delivered to your room free of charge. No need to choose between toting it all day (and maybe losing it or breaking it in the process) and having it delivered to the front of the park (where you'll have to stand in line at the end of the day to pick it up). You do have to allow 24 hours for the item to be delivered to your room, however, so you can't use this strategy the day you check out.

> *Note:* Be sure to check your packages when they arrive to see that everything is there and in good shape.

Helpful, knowledgeable staff

The staff in some hotels offsite could care less that Disney World is down the road. They could possibly give you directions on where to exit off the highway, but beyond that they aren't very helpful. In contrast, the WDW staff can give directions and advice. They can even help you plan your day. Just ask any employee you see. They are highly trained individuals who understand that you are truly a guest in their magical world.

Great atmosphere

Disney spares no expense when it comes to creating a great atmosphere. You will find well-themed and appointed buildings in every resort price range, set on grounds that meet or even exceed the theme parks' landscaping in their creativity and meticulous maintenance. A 35-foot Buzz Lightyear, the remains of a Mayan Temple, and four-story Southern mansions are among the features you will find at various WDW resorts. Disney understands that guests expect something out of the ordinary and they deliver. While you'll find nice resorts outside of WDW, none offer its unique variety of themed resorts.

Resort Issues

The expense, relatively small room size, and Disney's limit of four guests per room in most of its hotels are among the chief drawbacks to staying onsite.

Expense

WDW offers three types of properties, Value, Moderate, and Deluxe, as well as a campground. Rates for 2006 start at $79 for a standard room in a Value

Resort and $39 for a campground site in Value Season (see *Chapter One* for details on WDW seasons). The cost varies by season and location and is sometimes discounted — especially for Annual Passholders. The cheapest rate you are likely to find for a room on Disney property is around $60 a night in a Value Resort during the slowest time of the year, and there are no guarantees that such a huge discount will be offered in any given year.

Value Resort rooms are the same size as less expensive rooms you can get offsite for half the price. The Moderate and Deluxe Resorts are in a league of their own as far as price goes. Sometimes you can find rooms in a Moderate Resort for around $90 a night, but for many, that is still a steep price to pay for a bed, shower, and TV. You'll find details on specific resorts in the next chapter.

Rooms aren't "family" friendly

It may be harsh to say that Disney is not family friendly because Disney World was built for families. The problem isn't with the resorts themselves, but rather with the size of the rooms and the limits on the number of guests per room. Nearly all rooms on property accommodate no more than four guests (five if one is an infant, defined as age two or younger). We know there are a lot of families with four or fewer members, but there are also many with five or more. We happen to be one of them.

Many large families with small children are accustomed to bringing sleeping bags along when they travel and allowing the kids to sleep in them on the floor. That's not possible at Walt Disney World. Disney is strict about not letting more than four (five with an infant) stay in a Value Resort room. Since you have to register the names of everyone in your party (and the ages of any children in the party), you will be forced to get an extra room if you number more than four people age three or older. The Value Resorts offer no alternatives. If you want to stay onsite with a semi-large family (bigger than two adults and two children or one adult and three children), you have only three options: get two rooms, pay a lot for deluxe options, or camp.

> *Note:* A few Moderate Resort rooms in Port Orleans–Riverside accommodate five (six with an infant) and some Deluxe rooms accommodate six plus an infant, but their cost is prohibitive for guests on a tight budget.

In contrast, you'll find plenty of offsite options that offer the space you need at very modest rates. Many hotels offsite offer larger facilities for less, or just a little more, than the Value Resorts charge. Larger rooms with foldouts, multiple-room options, and special kid suites can be found offsite for $35 to $75 a night in Value Season. (See *Chapter Eight* for more on offsite lodging possibilities.)

No "free meals"

Disney does not offer its resort guests a complimentary continental breakfast or any discounts on food. There aren't any "kids eat free" or other such offers. Onsite guests pay the same for food as offsite guests who dine at Disney World.

> *Note:* You can get "free" meals with an upgraded package, but the reality is they are not free; you just pay for them in advance (see below).

No microwaves

If you'd like to heat food in your room, you'll be out of luck in most cases. The only resort rooms equipped with microwaves are in Deluxe Resorts and the Disney Vacation Club (DVC) timeshare properties. DVC units have kitchenettes and generally go for $100-plus a night when they're available. If you're staying anywhere else on site and wanted a microwave, you'd have to bring your own.

> *Note:* You might be able to buy DVC credits on eBay that would allow you to stay in one of these membership properties for under $100 a night, but there are no guarantees.

> *Tip:* If you don't mind the inconvenience, you can use the microwave in the food court at your resort. But this is awkward, time-consuming, and may make you uncomfortable.

Refrigerators cost extra at Value Resorts

Moderate and Deluxe Resort rooms offer free refrigerators. But if you're staying in a Value Resort, you'll be charged an extra $10 per night for a fridge ($10.60 with tax) unless you need it for medical reasons (to keep insulin, etc.). In that case, the refrigerator is free. Some Handicap Accessible rooms also come with a built-in fridge for free.

Hard to get offsite

Many people want to see all that the Orlando area has to offer — or at least Universal and SeaWorld. If you don't have a car, getting off property requires taking a taxi. But paying for a taxi defeats the goal of saving money. Not only will you have better access to Orlando's other attractions by staying off property, but also you can sometimes get better ticket deals for them through an offsite hotel (see *Chapter Eight*). Be aware that WDW transportation can only take you to Disney properties. The closest it comes to non-Disney venues is Downtown Disney, which offers some non-Disney shopping and restaurants.

Limited dining choices

When you stay onsite you don't have a lot of choices of where to eat. As a result, you end up spending more on meals out than you would if you were staying offsite and had access to a broader range of eating places. By making it hard to go off property, Disney can charge you a little more for basic food. It is the same at any ballpark or amusement park: no competition means higher prices.

Staying off property gives you more options for saving money. You not only have more freedom of choice, but also many offsite hotels offer you a free breakfast and/or discounts at their restaurants or restaurants nearby.

Limited or no last-minute bookings

You may have trouble getting a room at WDW at the last minute (or even a couple of months ahead), especially during Peak and Holiday Seasons. Disney is not supportive when it comes to guests who don't like to plan ahead. It likes to fill its rooms, dinner shows, character meals, etc. months in advance — or even a couple of years ahead in some cases. It only offers "last-minute" specials when bookings are slow — and even those must be booked as soon as you see them (see "Extra Tips," below).

Offsite hotels can get fully booked, too, especially at the holidays. On the whole, however, they not only welcome last-minute guests but also try to attract them with good deals. Keep this in mind if you don't like planning ahead.

There's such a thing as too much Disney

At the resorts you are exposed to the Disney magic 24/7, which can be too much for some to handle. For non-Disney fans who are making the trip for the sake of the kids, spouse, or friends, getting away from Disney at regular intervals makes the visit a whole lot more tolerable. While you won't have Disney music piped into your hotel room when you stay onsite, you will be immersed in the Disney atmosphere. It can be hard to detach yourself from the fantasy when you eat, sleep, and breathe it round-the-clock.

WDW Resort Categories

As mentioned above, Walt Disney World offers three categories of lodging: Value, Moderate, and Deluxe, plus a campground. The hotels in all categories are called resorts and their official names are all prefaced with the possessive, Disney's. The WDW property also includes three hotels (all in the Deluxe category) that are managed by companies other than Disney (Shades of Green, WDW Swan, and WDW Dolphin). We'll go into details in the next chapter. Here is an overview:

Value Resorts

(Disney's All-Star Movies, Music, and Sports, and Disney's Pop Century)

You'll pay $79 to $137 per night plus tax for a room in a Value Resort in 2006. This is definitely the cheapest way to stay on property. For the price, you will get a nice, clean room, but it will not be big and your door will open directly to the outdoors, just as it would in many motels. The theming for this category of hotels is very Disney — perfect for children. There are Disney characters everywhere, including larger than life statues and props scattered about the grounds.

> *$$aver Tip:* During Value Season and other select times of the year, Disney will often offer specials and discounts that bring the room price down to as little as $60 per night.

Moderate Resorts

(Disney's Caribbean Beach, Coronado Springs, Port Orleans–French Quarter, and Port Orleans–Riverside)

Rates for a Moderate Resort room in 2006 range from $139 to $215 per night before tax (and more for suites). These rooms are a little bigger than Value Resort rooms, but like them, sleep only four, with one exception: the Port Orleans–Riverside has a limited number of rooms that are equipped with hide-a-beds and can accommodate five. Coronado Springs, which houses WDW's onsite convention center, offers comfortable suite rooms. This is a great option if you have the bucks, but it is definitely not a money saver: you'll pay more for some suites than you would for two of the resort's standard rooms.

$$aver Tip: During Value Season and sporadically at other times, Disney offers standard Moderate Resort rooms for as little as $90 a night.

Deluxe Resorts / DVC

(Disney's Animal Kingdom Lodge, Beach Club, BoardWalk, Contemporary, Grand Floridian, Old Key West, Polynesian, Saratoga Springs, Wilderness Lodge, and Yacht Club, as well as Shades of Green (reserved for military personnel)

The 2006 rates for Deluxe rooms start at $205 to $359 before tax (depending on the hotel) — and that's in Value Season and without a preferred view. The rooms in these hotels are bigger than you will find in hotels in the other Resort categories, and most Deluxe resorts also offer suites. A big perk for guests is their proximity to a theme park. For example, you can walk to Epcot's back entrance gate in five minutes from Disney's BoardWalk Resort. Many swimming pools at these resorts have such elaborate themes that you will feel as though you are in a water park rather than a hotel pool.

$$aver Tip: During the Value Season and occasionally at other times, special discounts (mostly for Annual Passholders) can bring the price of a standard Deluxe room down to $135 a night.

Camping in Disney World

In 2006, Fort Wilderness Campground is charging $39 to $92 per night for a campground site that can accommodate up to 10 guests and $239 to $349 per night for a cabin that sleeps six. Camping is by far the most economical way to stay on property. If you enjoy camping and want to save money, this choice is a no-brainer.

Strategies for Saving on Resort Rooms

Pick the Right Start Date for Your Stay

Your room rate will depend on the day you start your vacation. Pick it carefully. If your first night is the last night of the Holiday Season and you stay for a week into the Value Season, your entire stay will be billed at the Holiday rate. This can also work in your favor. If your first night falls in the Value Season and you stay a week into the Holiday Season, your entire stay is billed at the Value rate. Here are some examples of how this could affect your bottom line:

• You are planning to stay at a Value Resort during the first week of January, one of the cheapest times of the year to visit Disney World. If you made reservations for December 31 (last day of the Holiday Season) through January 6, your rate would be $119 a night in a standard room, or $833 for the week before taxes and fees. However, if you reserved for January 1 to 7 instead, your rate for the same room would be $79 (or less) a night, or $553 for the week. By delaying your trip just one day, you'd save $280, and you'd probably be able to get any room you wanted.

• You've always wanted to spend the Christmas holidays at Disney World. You check Disney's web site and find that the Holiday Season begins December 20. You book your room for December 19 and stay through the most expensive time of the year at the cheapest rates.

> *$$aver Tip:* If you're coming for a week at Christmastime, consider making reservations that start the last day of the Value Season even if you can't arrive until a day or two later. Paying for an empty room for a night or two at the Value price might well cost you less than paying the premium price for the nights you're actually there. Call to verify that you will be late, but still want the room. This strategy is not guaranteed to work 100 percent of the time.

• You want to spend a long Christmas vacation at Disney World, arriving the 24th (during Holiday Season) and staying until January 6 (in Value Season). Consider making two reservations, one for each season. You pay Holiday rates for December 24 to 31 and Value Season rates for January 1 to 5. It's a little more work, but the work will pay off.

Don't Pay for a View

All Disney resorts offer preferred rooms. They give guests a better view or a location closer to the entrance of the hotel or the bus stop for a higher price. Do not take this option: you won't spend much time in the room, and almost every room offers a good view because the resorts were built so that parking lots are hidden, for the most part. Besides, the view from a preferred room often comes with a lot of noise because the room overlooks the pool and there is constant sound from children and families playing and splashing around.

> *Tip:* If a particular view or location is somewhat important to

you, always ask for a complimentary upgrade when you check in. You may feel awkward about this (at least at first), but it is perfectly OK and the Cast Member at reception won't be surly or snide. During slow times of the year, WDW might have many empty preferred rooms. In which case, the receptionist may be authorized to upgrade any guest who asks for one. Just be sure you stress the word "complimentary." If you simply ask to be upgraded, they might upgrade you and then charge you the preferred rate.

Caution: Watch out when you are booking a room on the WDW web site. The first quote that comes up is commonly for a preferred room (if they are available). This is how Disney can quickly and easily add at least another $12 a night to your expenses. Look at the other available options and choose a room that is not preferred. Better yet, don't book a room on the web site. You'll get a better deal by phoning.

Let Disney Help with the Financing: Book with Its CRO

When you book directly with Disney, the deal you get and the terms of your payment depend on which of Disney's two reservations desks you use when you make your booking, Disney's Central Reservation Office (CRO) or the Walt Disney Travel Company (WDTC). It is important that you book with the CRO. Here's why:

• **CRO terms.** When you book with the CRO you can make reservations as close as 14 days in advance of your stay, reserve your room with one night's deposit, and pay the rest when you check in. You can cancel or change your reservations up to five days before check-in without a penalty. If you cancel within five days of your stay, you will pay a cancellation fee equal to the cost of one night's stay.

• **WDTC terms.** Compared with those terms, the WDTC terms put you at a big disadvantage. WDTC requires a $200 deposit and full payment 45 days before check-in. If you book less than 45 days in advance, you may have to pay for your entire stay when you make your reservation. WDTC's cancellation policy is also harsher, and the terms can be especially onerous for Value Resort guests. If you cancel 6 to 45 days before arrival, WDTC charges a $100 cancellation fee. The fee soars to $200 if you cancel within five days of arrival. That's more than the cost of two nights in a Value Resort standard room during the Value and Regular Seasons. (Of course, if you booked in the Deluxe category, you would come out better under WDTC cancellation terms.)

>*Caution:* You must phone to book through the CRO. When you book online with Disney, your booking is automatically handled by the WDTC. Therefore, be sure to call (407-WDISNEY) and ask to be connected to someone in the Central Reservation Office. The payment terms and the offers they provide can make a big difference in how long your money stays in your pocket, as well as how much you'll have to pay if you should have to cancel or change your reservation. Let Disney help you with the financing.

Stay at Shades of Green if You Can

This top-notch resort, located by three WDW golf courses and fairly close to the Magic Kingdom, is owned by the Department of Defense and reserved exclusively for the enjoyment of military, Department of Defense, and Public Health Service personnel and their families and friends. If you qualify, you can stay in a Deluxe Resort at Value Resort prices. You have to be, or be married to, an active or reserve duty member of the armed forces or National Guard, or other qualified person, to book a room at Shades of Green. You can reserve up to three rooms if you qualify.

>*$$aver Tip:* Inquire about any and all military discounts Disney may be offering. It often has discounts for active military and reservists, but it doesn't always announce them. Ask.

Do the Room-Rate Math

If your group or family wants to stay at Disney World but is large enough to require more than one standard room, consider your options carefully. The easy option would be to get two rooms at a Value Resort. This works out well for eight people, but for five, six, or seven there may be better options. It could be cheaper for a group of five (six with an infant) to book a single room at Port Orleans Riverside, a Moderate Resort with some rooms that accommodate five (see the following chapter). Bigger groups may want to consider camping.

Share a Campsite with Friends

Up to ten people can share the same Fort Wilderness campsite and put up multiple tents for an additional charge of just $2 per adult camper per night (for more than two adults). If you enjoy camping (or are willing to give it a try), you could split a site with your extended family, another family, or a group of friends and save a lot of money.

Consider Buying at Least One Annual Pass

When booking a resort, look at the potential savings to be had with an Annual Pass. Disney offers frequent discounts to Annual Passholders, and only one person in your party needs to have one to qualify for the discount. You can reserve up to three rooms on one Annual Pass per stay.

Sometimes the cost of buying that one Annual Pass is negligible in comparison to the huge savings it can bring. If Disney offers Annual Passholders a $30 discount on a room and you need the room for seven nights, that's a savings of $210 on the room. An Annual Pass costs $395 (just $167 more than a five-day ticket with a Hopper option). You'd net $43 in savings after paying for your pass — and that's just for starters. The pass entitles you to discounts on WDW food and merchandise. It also allows you to visit Disney World as many times as you can within the next 12 months.

> *Note:* If you were traveling with a group of friends, you could save as much as $630 on three rooms during your week's stay with a $30 per night per room discount — or $235 after deducting the cost of the Annual Pass. A small group can save money, a large one can save even more!

> *Caution:* Remember, if you book using an Annual Pass rate, your reservations will be for the room only. Others in your party will have to have their own Annual Passes or tickets to enter the theme parks.

Straight Talk on Disney Packages

Buying a package that includes hotel and airfare, or hotel, airfare, and a car rental can definitely save you money, as we discussed in *Chapter Two*. You can buy these packages on your own, through web sites such as Expedia.com, or get them through a travel agent. But there's another type of package that bears very close examination, Disney's Magic Your Way packages. At their most basic, they combine a stay in a WDW resort hotel with admission tickets to the theme parks. The priciest ones add on a meal plan plus just about anything you could possibly do at WDW.

There is no question that they are convenient. The question is, are they worth the money?

> *Note:* When calculating lodging charges, Disney classifies children ages 10 to 17 as "Juniors." Juniors can stay in a room with their parents at no extra charge. However, they are still classified as "Adults" when calculating ticket prices and charges for other activities. You do not have to buy a Magic Your Way resort package to take advantage of the Junior classification for children age 10 to 17.

Can You Use All You Pay For?

Disney packages include admission tickets for your arrival and departure days, for example, "7 days/ 6 nights." In reality, most people can get only five days in the parks out of a six-night stay. If you fly in, chances are you won't get in, and then into your room, until late in the afternoon. Even if you make it to the parks, you won't be there the whole day; but you will pay for the whole day if you buy a package.

The same goes for your departure day. By the time you have repacked and budgeted the time to get to the airport and get through security (or to get on the road in time to make the most of daylight driving hours), you probably won't have time to go to the parks. So you will have wasted two days of admission.

On the other hand, unless you choose to add the No Expiration option to your tickets, a seven-day ticket costs only $5 (child) to $6 (adult) more than a five-day ticket, or $22 for a family of two adults and two children. Still, that's about enough for a meal at a counter service restaurant.

You May Not Save a Cent

Disney boasts that a family of four can stay for a week (7 days/ 6 nights) for under $1,500. The sample package they offered included a Value Resort room and a seven-day base ticket for each family member. We tested it online for a typical family of four, two adults and two children (ages three to nine). The price was, as promised, under $1,500 ($1,438.26 plus tax*). This was based on $77 a night at a Value Resort (the Value Season rate in 2005). If you price the components yourself, you'll see that the savings just aren't there.

> *Note:* The examples opposite are based on Value Season pricing. Add $120 to the room cost for stays in Regular Season.

The Package "Benefits" Are Nothing Special

Don't be fooled by the benefits that Disney lists as part of its package. You can get the exact same benefits (Magical Express service, Extra Magic Hours, and free use of WDW transportation), at the exact same price, by booking a room at any WDW resort and booking your tickets separately.

Disney's Sample 7-Day Package	
Value Resort Room in Value Season ($77 x 6)	= $462.00
2 Adult 7-day base tickets	= $398.00
2 Child 7-day base tickets	= $320.00
Total cost (before tax)	**= $1,180.00**

*Disney's quoted price was $1,438.26. We still don't know where the other $258.26 went.

If you are willing to spend $1,400 on your vacation, you can stay longer and still spend under $1,500:

Our 10-Day "Package"	
Value Resort Room in Value Season ($77 x 9)	= $693.00
2 Adult 7-day passes	= $398.00
2 Child 7-day passes	= $320.00
Total cost (before tax)	**= $1,411.00**

With our "package," you can stay at WDW nine nights (ten days) and actually enjoy the parks for seven *full* days!

Premium Tickets Aren't Worth the Money

You can upgrade a Magic Your Way package to include the Disney Dining Experience plan and Premium tickets. Don't do it. The dining plan (see *Chapter Three*) is a little too much for most guests to handle. It could be a good deal if your family eats a lot, but if not, you're better off paying as you go. The Premium upgrade doubles the cost of the basic package and includes tickets to almost every option available at Walt Disney World. The kicker is that no one has enough time to do everything at WDW in under a month, and most people wouldn't be interested in doing everything even if they could. Unlimited golf, free tours, and tickets to all of the major and minor parks sounds great, but you won't have time to do them all. Pay-as-you-go is still the best way, even if you plan to do as many extra things as you can fit in.

Extra Onsite Hotel Tips from "Disney on a Dime"

Look for Disney specials. From time to time, Disney offers some very special deals — seven nights for the price of four or five, for example. Such deals offer a great savings. If you find one, take a hard look at it to see if it could work for you. Typically deals like these are offered for stays in the latter part of the summer or for the fall. Check our web site, www.disneyonadime.com, to see what's on offer currently. We'll try to keep you up to date on all the latest opportunities to save.

Waiting sometimes pays. This may sound like a contradiction of our "no last-minute bookings" comment, above. However, if you are looking to go in late April or May (except Memorial Day weekend) or between mid-September and mid-November, you may be better off waiting until a couple of months before your trip to book your room. Disney commonly discounts heavily in April, May, August, and September. Discounts aren't published until a month or two before they take effect.

This strategy carries some risk, of course, because crowds could be above normal and the discounts might not materialize, but there isn't a high risk of ending up with no room at these times.

> *Note:* Don't wait if you're looking to book at other times of the year. Doing so is extremely risky in other seasons because the resorts fill up then.

Do the Annual Pass calculus. Annual Pass rates are generally the best available. The trick is to see if the Annual Pass deals currently on offer will make it worth your while to purchase an Annual Pass. To view the latest Passholder deals without first purchasing a pass, you will have to go to a non-Disney site, such as www.disneyonadime.com or allearsnet.com, because Disney's web site requires that you type in the code on your Annual Pass before you can see the Passholder rates. Look for all of the deals and specials that Disney is offering and then make your decision.

Book now, buy an Annual Pass later. Most people do not realize that they can book a room under an Annual Pass discount before they actually buy an Annual Pass. If it will work out to your advantage, go ahead and book the room and then buy an Annual Pass before you leave on your trip. You will need your pass at check-in, but not before.

> *Note:* As we go to press, Disney is experimenting with a program that would allow Passholders to book Disney's "Best Rate" 90 days in advance. This would entitle the Passholder to get the better deal if the prices went down after the Passholder booked. Word of mouth so far indicates that the test isn't delivering to either Disney's or Passholders' expectations.

Book now, re-book later. If having a reservation makes you feel more secure, book now and then re-book if a better deal comes along. Reserve your room through Disney's Central Reservations Office (or CRO, see above) or a travel agent who specializes in Walt Disney World (see below). Then keep a lookout for any special offers or better deals. If you find one, ask to have your reservations changed. If that doesn't work, check to be sure you can cancel without penalty, and then book the new deal and cancel your first reservation.

> *Tip:* Always be sure you can book the new offer before you cancel your existing reservation and always check the cancellation policy before you cancel. The deals Disney puts out are sometimes so limited that they can sell out before most people even hear about them. In other cases, the penalty you'd have to pay for canceling would eliminate any benefits of a lower rate (see below).

Can't get in where you want? Ask for a complimentary upgrade. If the hotel you had your heart set on is full, ask for a complimentary upgrade to a preferred room in another hotel in the same category or to a hotel in a higher category. When Disney is overbooked in one resort category, it often has plenty of openings in resorts in other categories; so asking to be bumped up is a very wise strategy. A lot of times, the operator is authorized either to fill a certain number of Moderate or Deluxe resort rooms at the lower rate you would have paid in the resort that's booked up or to meet you halfway. Ask and see what happens. You might get your wish.

> *Note:* The operator won't volunteer complimentary upgrade information. You have to ask.

Consider resort hopping. If you'd like to stay in the "lap of luxury," but can't afford five nights or a week at a Moderate or Deluxe Resort and if you don't mind moving around during your stay, reserve rooms in two different resorts. For example, you could spend three nights at a Value or Moderate Resort followed by two nights at a Moderate or Deluxe Resort. Disney will transport your luggage from one to the other for free. All you will have to do is pack and unpack everything in the middle of your trip. Better yet, pack separate bags for each resort.

> *Note:* You will have to make two separate reservations because Disney's reservations system will not put two different resorts under one reservation.

> *$$aver Tip:* Time your stay at the Deluxe property for a week-night; the prices are generally lower than on weekends. Moderate and Value Resorts, however, typically charge the same rates every day of the week.

Use a travel agent who specializes in Disney vacations. We can't stress this enough. Travel agencies that don't specialize just don't know enough about the available options to get you the best deal for your own particular needs and desires. Disney specialists like Kingdom Konsultants, Mouse Ear Vacations, Second Star Vacations, and Small World Vacations are very price conscious and will work with you to ensure a truly magical vacation that suits your family and your budget. See "Consult Some Travel Agents" in *Chapter Two* for more details.)

Sign up for everything Walt Disney World offers. When WDW gives you a chance to join a club or get an offer, sign up for it. This is a great way to broaden your chances of winning a free trip or other prizes. By getting into Disney's database you will be more likely to receive special offers and discount codes. Disney often mails out special offers that can be used only by the recipient. In 2004, we received a discount in the mail for a $49 special on Value Resort rooms during "Regular Season" (a $99 value). Sign up for Disney mailing lists at www.disneyworld.com and www.disneydirect.com.

How to Take Full Advantage of Your First and Last Ticket Days When You Buy a Package

The big problem with a Magic Your Way package is that it forces you to buy two admission days that you probably won't be able to use (see "Straight Talk on Disney Packages," above). Here's a strategy that will let you take full advantage of those ticket days. It will work best for those who plan to drive to Walt Disney World, rent a car at the airport, or fly into an airport other than Orlando International (see "Trade-off," below):

> *$$aver Tip:* Stay offsite at a really cheap hotel on your days of arrival and departure.

On arrival day

Pick up any groceries you need (see Chapters *Three* and *Nine*) and then check into to your offsite hotel. Spend any free time you may have exploring Downtown Disney or taking in one of Orlando's minor attractions. Get up early the next morning, eat the free breakfast (if offered), and then check out of your offsite hotel and into your WDW resort hotel. You can check-in as early as you want. Just leave your bags and a Cast Member will take them to your room when it becomes available. Now head right for the park of your choice and take full advantage of the first ticket day of your Disney package.

> *Note:* You probably won't have access your WDW room until mid or late afternoon; so pack anything you'll need to carry into the park with you (sunscreen, drinks, diapers, camera, etc.) in a backpack, cooler, or tote before you leave the offsite hotel so that you're ready to roll as soon as you've checked in at your resort.

On your last ticket day

Check out of your resort hotel and put your bags in your car. Enjoy your day in the theme park. Your ticket is good till the park closes. When you leave for the day, go to an offsite hotel for the night and depart for home in the morning.

Trade-off

When you use this strategy, you will not be able to take advantage of Disney's free Magical Express shuttle service between Orlando International Airport and your Disney World resort. If you plan to fly into Orlando International and do not plan to rent a car, do not use this strategy. You will spend a lot more on an airport shuttle service than you will lose by not taking advantage of all your ticket days.

SAVE ON LODGING
Part 2: Affordable WDW Hotels

Budget-conscious guests can find reasonable accommodations on property. The rooms will cost more than you would pay for similar accommodations offsite, but they will offer all the benefits discussed in *Chapter Six*.

This chapter will focus on WDW's Value and Moderate resorts, along with the Fort Wilderness Campground, which represents an especially good value. At $205 to $2,500 per night (before tax), the Deluxe resorts are not very affordable and do not fit the bill for going to Walt Disney World on a budget.

The Basics

Wherever you stay on property, some general rules apply:

Standard room rates

Rates in all WDW Resort rooms are based on two adults in a room. Kids under 18 stay free in a room with a paying adult. However, any child 18 or older is considered an adult and Disney charges an additional $12 to $15 per adult per night for the third and fourth adults in a room.

> *Note:* This is the one place on WDW property where Disney gives parents a break in defining an "adult." You'll still have to buy adult admission tickets for everyone in your party who is 10 or older.

Kids stay free only if the family is small enough

Disney places strict limits on the total number of guests per room. If you need an extra room for the kids, you will, of course, have to pay for it.

Only four to a room

As discussed in *Chapter Six*, the rooms in the Value and Moderate resorts (a few rooms in Port Orleans Riverside excepted) accommodate a maximum of four guests (five if one is an infant, i.e., age two or younger). If you need more space, your only options in these resort categories are to book additional rooms, get a suite at Coronado Springs (expensive), or opt for a campsite instead. Keep this in mind when you calculate the costs of staying onsite.

Laundry facilities

You'll find coin laundry facilities at each resort. The cost for the machines, as we go to press, is $2.00 per washer load and $2.00 for 30 minutes of dryer time. Laundry detergent is available for about $3.50; the little box has enough for about three loads. All Disney resorts also offer laundry pick-up services daily except Sundays and holidays. Services and prices vary from resort to resort. Your Guest Services desk can fill you in.

Value Resorts

(2006 Rates $79 to $137)

Disney offers four Value Resorts to its most money-conscious guests, the three All-Star Resorts (Movies, Music, and Sports) and the Pop Century. Staying at a Value Resort is not exactly what you'd call super inexpensive, but it is cheaper than all other on-site options except camping at Fort Wilderness Campgrounds (see below). The accommodations are what you would expect from a general chain hotel — no big frills, just nice, clean, convenient rooms with some Disney magic and special swimming pools thrown in for good measure. For the money and the location, they are good enough.

All the rooms in the Value Resorts accommodate four people (five if one is an infant). The buildings are more motel-like than resort-like, but the rooms are creatively decorated and with plenty of Disney theming to add a little class to the structures. The rates are same at all four resorts.

The All-Star Resorts (Movies, Music, and Sports)

Each All-Star Resort consists of ten themed buildings. The buildings are essentially three-story, T-shaped motels. They open directly to the outside and each is equipped with two elevators, centrally located in the middle of the "T." There are stairwells at the ends. If your room is too far from the elevators to make the walk worthwhile, you can always use the stairs.

Each Resort has two well-themed swimming pools and a food court offering counter service for breakfast, lunch, and dinner, along with a small grocery store, a bakery, and a grill. Other amenities include an arcade, gift-shop, and playground. Some buildings in each resort are closer to the food court and bus stops than others (see below).

While you are not guaranteed rooms in a particular building when you make your booking, you can ask reservations to note your preference. If it's available when you check in, you'll get it.

> *Exception*: If you pay for a preferred room, you know that you will be in a particular area, but it will cost you a minimum of $12 extra per night.

> *Note:* A downside to staying in the All-Star Resorts is that they are located a good distance from the theme parks.

All-Star Resorts quick facts and tips

Each resort has 1,920 rooms.

Rates for 2006: $79 for a standard room in Value Season to $137 for a preferred room in Holiday Season, based on two adults.

$10 per night additional for each additional adult.

Preferred rooms available for $12 per night more than a standard room.

Maximum occupancy: four persons per room (five if one is an infant).

Each room is approximately 260 square feet.

Most rooms have two double beds; some have one king-sized bed.

Phone with voicemail, iron, and ironing board are standard in every room.

Hair dryers and cribs are available free of charge.

Refrigerators are available for $10 a night.

Babysitting and child-care are available.

You can have pizza delivered.

Disney's All-Star Movies Resort

The All-Star Movies Resort is a favorite among children. You can stay in hotel buildings themed after *101 Dalmatians*, *Toy Story*, *Mighty Ducks*, *Fantasia*, and *Herbie: The Love Bug*. The hotels use characters from these movies to make some very impressive décor. You'll find larger than life monuments based on these Disney classics around all the buildings. For example, a 35-foot Buzz Lightyear and a 25-foot Woody near the Toy Story buildings will get any *Toy Story* fan excited. Inside, the rooms are decorated with curtains, bed-spreads, and pictures that continue the movie themes. All-Star Movies' food court is called World Premier, and its nicely sized pools are themed after *The Mighty Ducks* and *Fantasia*. The Mighty Ducks pool includes a huge Duck hockey mask surrounded by gigantic hockey sticks. The Fantasia pool has a statue of Mickey Mouse and a kiddie pool with a baby whale surrounded by icebergs from *Fantasia 2000*.

The buildings:

101 Dalmatians buildings are #1 and #4. They're decorated with huge statues of Perdy and Pongo with little Dalmatians running everywhere.

Toy Story buildings are #9 and #10. Statues of Buzz (#10) and Woody (#9) guard these buildings with a couple of Buckets O' Soldiers protecting the perimeter.

Fantasia buildings are #5 and #8. A magical hat and a walking broom decorate the regular Fantasia (#5) building grounds, while a jack-in-the-box is located in front of the Fantasia 2000 (#8) building.

Warning to parents with small children: The jack-in-the-box looks a little sinister and could frighten some kids.

The Mighty Ducks buildings are #2 and #3. Hockey sticks and Duck masks surround these buildings.

Herbie: The Love Bug buildings are #6 and #7. A regular-sized Herbie and a much bigger replica are surrounded by 25-foot tools.

More tips:

• Don't get the preferred rooms unless you need to be by the Fantasia pool and a little closer to the main building. Remember, a preferred room is at least $12 extra per night. You can always ask for a complimentary upgrade when you check in.

• If you want to be closer to the bus stop, try to get into the Toy Story or 101 Dalmatians buildings.

• If your children are at that "magical age," try to get into the Toy Story, 101 Dalmatians, or Fantasia buildings. They might not know or be very impressed by Herbie: The Love Bug or The Mighty Ducks themes.

Disney's All-Star Music Resort

The All-Star Music Resort, located between the All-Star Movies and All-Star Sports Resorts, offers the most adult theming of the three All-Star resorts. Like All-Star Movies, it offers five themes, in this case, Calypso, Country Fair, Jazz Inn, Rock Inn, and Broadway Hotel. Instead of gigantic characters, musical instruments and icons three or more stories high adorn the landscape. A huge fiddle or a jukebox that is out of this world are among the ornaments you can expect to see here.

The All-Star Music Resort calls its food court Intermission. One of its pools is shaped like a piano complete with the piano keys and a statue of Ariel and friends. The other is the Calypso pool. It is shaped like a guitar and has a statue of Donald and the gang from *Saludos Amigos* spraying water out of their guns. Next to the Calypso pool you'll find a small wading pool that is perfect for the kids.

The buildings:

Calypso buildings are #1 and #10. They have a very festive feel with 30-foot maracas and bongo drums decorating the area.

Jazz Inn buildings are #2 and #9. A huge drum set and the silhouette of Louis Armstrong mark these buildings.

Rock Inn buildings are #3 and #4. Here you'll see a giant jukebox and guitar.

Country Fair buildings are #5 and #6. The grounds sport a monumental fiddle, banjo, and cowboy boots.

Broadway Hotel buildings are #7 and #8. A street going through the middle of these buildings sports a marquee advertising "Beauty and the Beast" and gives you the feel of being on the Great White Way.

More tips:

• The only buildings that are close to the front and to the bus stop are the Calypso buildings.

• Don't get the preferred rooms unless you need to be by the Calypso pool and a little closer to the main building. Remember, a preferred room is at least $12 extra per night.

Disney's All-Star Sports Resort .

The All-Star Sports Resort is adjacent to the All-Star Music Resort and is decorated with exaggerated sports equipment and themes. Here you will find names like Touchdown!, Center Court, Homerun Hotel, Surf's Up!, and Hoops Hotel. This Resort would probably be a good fit for families with teens and tweens. The theme here is less cartoon-like than the All-Star Movies' theme and not as grown-up as the All-Star Music theme; so it fills that middle ground.

The rooms in this resort are creatively decorated with sports-themed curtains, bedspreads, and pictures, while the buildings sport touches like 40-foot tennis rackets with tennis ball containers for stairwells and baseball bats longer than a bus.

You can grab a bite to eat at the End Zone Food Court and swim in the Surfboard Bay and the Grand Slam pools. The Surfboard Bay pool is humorously themed with huge shark fins encircling the water. The Grand Slam pool is shaped like a baseball diamond, complete with a backstop, bases, and a statue of Goofy in the middle of the pool shooting water out of a cannon.

The buildings:

Surf's Up! buildings are #1 and #6. They are decorated with surfboards, surfboards, and more surfboards.

Hoops Hotel buildings are #2 and #3. Look for big basketballs, hoops, and huge whistles in the stairwells.

Center Court buildings are #4 and #5. Tennis rackets, tennis balls, and a "tennis court" identify these buildings.

Touchdown! buildings are #7 and #10. Goal posts and a football field with x's and o's dot the landscape.

Home Run Hotel buildings are #8 and #9. You'll feel like you are in a ballpark stadium.

More tips:

• Don't get the preferred rooms unless you need to be by the Surfboard Bay pool and a little closer to the main building. Remember, a preferred room is at least $12 extra per night.

• If you want to be closer to the bus stop, try to get into the Touchdown! buildings.

• The Hoops Hotel and the Center Court buildings are the farthest away from everything (the entrance, food court, and pools).

Disney's Pop Century Resort

(Rates for 2006: $79 to $137)

The Pop Century Resort is WDW's newest Value Resort and by far the biggest. The hotel, only halfway completed due to a reduction in guests in the months following 9/11, is located near Disney's Wide World of Sports Complex, rather than near the other three Value Resorts. So far, it consists of ten large buildings themed to five decades, the 1950s, 1960s, 1970s, 1980s, and 1990s. The final phase will add another ten buildings (themed to the first five decades of the twentieth century), with an hourglass lake dividing the first half of the century from the last.

Buildings at Pop Century are similar to those at the other Value Resorts, except that they are four stories high instead of three. There are elevators in each building, but if you are in a hurry and would prefer to take the stairs rather than wait to ride, you'll find climbing a bit more of a chore if your room is located on the fourth floor.

These hotels are meant to take you back to a place in your recent past or your childhood (or your parents' childhoods). Pop Century has far more diverse figures and objects on the outside of its buildings than the other Value Resorts. It is virtually littered with icons to help you visualize the hits of the past decades — 40-foot eight-track tape players, a Rubik's cube, a cell phone, and a laptop computer are the types of things you will see here. The rooms echo the decades' theme with wallpaper, bedspreads, and curtains specific to their respective decades.

The Pop Century Resort includes three pools to accommodate the extra guests that come with its buildings' extra floor. The Seventies' Hippy Dippy Pool looks like something right out of *Laugh-in*. It is flower-shaped with silhouettes of dancers all around it and a kiddie pool close by. The Bowling Pin Pool is shaped like a bowling pin, of course, and is set in the Fifties' era. The Computer Pool is set in the Eighties and comes complete with its own "soft keyboard" — a kiddie pool with rubberized flooring.

You can grab a bite to eat at the Food Court, which offers counter service for breakfast, lunch, and dinner, as well as a small grocery store, bakery, and grill. Other amenities include an arcade, a gift shop, a nice playground, and a children's water play area where a Goofy fixture can splash them.

Quick facts and tips

Pop Century has 2,880 rooms now (960 more than at each of the other Value

Resorts) and will have 5,760 when completed.

Rates for 2006: $79 for a standard room in Value Season to $137 for a preferred room in Holiday Season, based on two adults.

$10 per night additional for each additional adult.

Preferred rooms available for $12 per night more than a standard room.

Maximum occupancy: four persons per room (five if one is an infant).

Each room is approximately 260 square feet.

Most rooms have two double beds; some have one king-sized bed.

Phone with voicemail, iron, and ironing board are standard in every room.

Hair dryers and cribs are available free of charge.

Babysitting and childcare are available.

Refrigerators are available for $10 a night.

You can have pizza delivered.

The buildings:

'50s has three buildings. They are decorated with a jukebox, bowling pins, and Lady and the Tramp.

'60s has two buildings. Look for Play-Doh, yo-yo's, and Baloo and Mowgli from the *Jungle Book*.

'70s has two buildings. A Mickey Mouse telephone, a huge Big Wheel, Foosball players, and an eight-track tape player are the icons here.

'80s has two buildings. A Rubik's cube and a Walkman mark this decade.

'90s has just one building. Its icons are a cellular phone and a laptop computer.

More tips:

• If you want to be closer to the bus stop, try the '70s buildings.

• Don't get the preferred rooms unless you need to be by the Hippy Dippy Pool and a little closer to the main building. Remember, a preferred room is at least $12 extra per night.

Moderate Resorts

(2006 Rates $139 - $1,170)

A Moderate Resort is a great place to stay if you want to do a little more than simply go to the theme parks. The Moderate Resorts are a fairly big step up from the Value Resorts. While the Value Resorts are fine places to stay and have great themes, they are not particularly resort-like. The Moderate Resorts offer a resort atmosphere and have a better overall feel than the Value Resorts. They are situated on spacious grounds and offer bigger rooms and more amenities, including sit-down restaurants and spectacular swimming pools. As a result, you have more opportunities to relax and enjoy your vacation. The sit-down restaurants make dining convenient for Moderate Resort guests who have to eat out in order to feel that they are on vacation.

Quick Facts and Tips

Rates for 2006: from $139 for a standard room in Value Season to $1,170 for a two-bedroom suite at Coronado Springs Resort in Holiday Season, based on two adults. The standard room rate in Holiday Season is $189.

$15 per night additional for each additional adult.

Extra charge of $16 (in Value Season) to $26 (in Holiday Season) for rooms with king-size beds.

Maximum occupancy: four persons per room (five if one is an infant), except for some rooms in Port Orleans Riverside and some suites in Coronado Springs (see below).

Each room is over 300 square feet.

Most rooms have two full-size beds; about 60 in each resort have a king-size bed.

Phone with voicemail and data ports, hair dryer, iron, ironing board, coffee maker, and refrigerator are standard in each room.

Cribs are available free of charge.

Babysitting and child-care services are available.

Limited room service available.

Guests can rent boats for $7 to $25 per half-hour: $7 for paddle boats, which hold up to four people; $21 for a Water Mouse speedboat, which accommodates two, and $25 for a canopy boat, which can seat eight.

Bicycle rentals are available for about $8 an hour, $22 per day.

> *$$aver Tip:* Throughout the year, Disney offers discounts to Annual Passholders and to the general public, bringing the room cost down to as low as $85 a night. Watch for these special deals and you may be able to stay at a Moderate Resort for just a little more money than you'd pay at a Value Resort. Deals like these can save you over $300 a week on a standard Moderate Resort room.

Disney's Caribbean Beach Resort

The Caribbean Beach Resort is fairly big and disconnected. It is divided into six different villages (Barbados, Martinique, Aruba, Jamaica, Trinidad North, and Trinidad South) plus a central activity area called Old Port Royale. The villages are spread out all over the resort and surround a 45-acre lake called Barefoot Bay. The roominess allows you to relax and enjoy the Caribbean atmosphere.

Unlike the hotels in the Value Resorts, the villages at the Caribbean Beach are part of a single, unified theme. Each village has a white sand beach, a pool, and six buildings, except Trinidad North, which has only three buildings. The buildings are two-story structures with hallways. There are no elevators, so if you think you will have trouble getting up and down stairs, you will need to request a room on the ground floor. Preferred room options are determined by view, rather than location. If you want a lake view, you must request a preferred room.

Old Port Royale, the central activity area, houses the main building, food court, sit-down restaurant (Shutters), small grocery market, gift shop, and a huge themed pool. The pool, designed to resemble a Spanish Fort, has waterfalls, water slides, and water cannons. The cannons line a bridge that crosses the pool and slides; they are great fun for the kids. There is a wading pool close by, along with a whirlpool.

Quick facts and tips

The Caribbean Beach has 2,112 rooms.

Each room is approximately 340 square feet.

Every village has its own pool in addition to sharing the one in Port Royale.

The buildings:

Barbados Village includes buildings #11 through #16.

Martinique Village includes buildings #21 through #26.

Trinidad North Village includes buildings #31 through #33.

Trinidad South Village includes buildings #34 through #39.

Jamaica Village includes buildings #41 through #46.

Aruba Village includes buildings #51 through #56.

More tips:

• Every village has its own bus stop.

• The villages closest to the main building (Old Port Royale) are Martinique and Trinidad North. The villages farthest away are Barbados and Trinidad South. Due to the size of the resort your location can make a huge difference in convenience when it comes to eating. From Barbados or Trinidad South you may need to walk half a mile or take the bus to get to the central food court and restaurant.

Disney's Coronado Springs Resort

The theme at Coronado Springs Resort ranges from Spanish colonial to Mexico and the American Southwest as you move from Cabanas, to Casitas, to Ranchos. While each of the three areas has its own swimming pool, they share the huge Mayan Pyramid Pool. The pool lies at the base of what looks to be a genuine Mayan Temple in an area called the Dig Site. Other components of the Site include a long water slide, children's pool, sand box, spa, arcade, and playground. El Centro, the main building, houses such amenities as a hairstyling salon, health club, and convenience store.

Coronado Springs offers a variety of dining options: a counter-service food court (Pepper Market), a casual lounge (Francisco's) offering light appetizers, and a sit-down restaurant (Maya Grill) that serves breakfast and dinner.

The resort houses WDW's only moderately priced convention center, complete with meeting rooms, a full business center, and a main ballroom that can accommodate 5,000 guests for dinner. If you are thinking of staying at Coronado Springs, keep in mind that you are likely to be sharing the property with several thousand conventioneers and meeting attendees.

Quick facts and tips

Coronado Springs has 1,967 rooms.

Standard rooms are approximately 314 square feet.

Some multi-room suites can accommodate several guests, which is the reason the rate range is so wide at this resort.

$$aver Tip: It can be cheaper to stay in two rooms than to get a suite.

Wireless (Wi-Fi) Internet service is available for $9.95 for continuous 24-hour service.

Every area has its own bus stop.

The buildings:

The Casitas are located closest to the convention center and the resort's restaurants and shops. These three- and four-story buildings are designed specifically for convention guests.

The Cabanas are two-story structures that bring to mind the coasts of Mexico. Most of them have a lake view and the whole area has a sandy shoreline along the lake. The buildings are fairly close to the convention center and the shops located in the main building.

The Ranchos are two- and three-story buildings that have a pueblo/desert feel to them. The landscaping includes rocks, sand, and cacti. This group of buildings is the farthest from the main buildings, but the closest to the resort's spectacular main pool.

More tips:

• Due to the size of the resort, your location can make a huge difference in the convenience of eating. From some areas of the resort you may need to walk half a mile or take the bus to get to the food court or restaurant.

• Don't get the preferred rooms unless you want a lake view. Remember, a preferred room is at least $15 extra per night.

• The buildings closest to El Centro, the main building, are the Casitas and the Cabanas.

• The Ranchos are the farthest from the restaurants and El Centro and the closest to the Mayan Pyramid Pool.

Disney's Port Orleans Resorts

In 2001, Disney combined its Port Orleans Resort with its Dixie Landings Resort to create Port Orleans–French Quarter and Port Orleans–Riverside. The two are close enough together that guests at either one can enjoy the restaurants, pools, and amenities of the other.

Port Orleans–French Quarter

French Quarter is the smaller of the two Port Orleans Resorts. Built to re-create New Orleans' French Quarter, it is a cleaner, tamer version of the real deal that still manages to create the feel of being in the "Big Easy." French Quarter has a Mardi Gras theme. Large carnival masks and instrument-playing animals decorate the property, but the theming isn't over-the-top as it is at the Value Resorts.

There are seven hotel buildings in French Quarter. The buildings do not have fanciful names, just numbers (1 through 7). Each is three stories high and opens directly to the outdoors. The resort has only one pool, Doubloon Lagoon, but it's a winner. It features a huge serpent slide, Jacuzzi, and alligator fountains. A counter-service food court called the Sassagoula Floatworks and Food Factory serves breakfast, lunch, and dinner. Other amenities include an arcade and a playground.

French Quarter quick facts and tips

French Quarter has 1,000 rooms.

Each room is approximately 314 square feet.

Rates range from $139 for a standard room in Value Season to $215 for a preferred room in Holiday Season.

The buildings:

The buildings closest to the main building are #2, #3, #4, and #5.

The buildings bordering the river are #1, #2, #5, #6, and #7.

The buildings around the pool are #2 and #5.

The buildings farthest away from the main building are #1, #6, and #7.

More Tips:

• There is one bus stop for the whole resort, but the resort isn't as expansive as the other Moderate Resorts.

• Don't get the preferred rooms unless you want a river view. Remember, a preferred room is at least $15 extra per night.

Port Orleans–Riverside

The Riverside Resort was known as Dixie Landings until 2001 when it was combined with Disney's Port Orleans Resort and renamed. Riverside's award-winning grounds are immaculate and some would say they are the best on property.

The resort captures the look of the Old South along the Mississippi. It is divided into two areas, Alligator Bayou and Magnolia Bend. Each has its own theme and "housing" style. The 16 two-story buildings on the Alligator Bayou side of the resort evoke the downtowns of the old South and have no elevators. The four buildings on the Magnolia Bend side look like huge southern mansions. These four-story buildings come with elevators and are named Acadian House, Magnolia Terrace, Oak Manor, and Parterre Place.

Port Orleans Riverside has five heated pools scattered among the buildings (three in Alligator Bayou and two in Magnolia Bend) plus a big pool on Ol' Man Island, which is centrally located between the Bayou and the Bend. The big pool has a slide, kiddie pool, Jacuzzi, wading pool, and a geyser. A sit-down restaurant called Boatwright's Dining Hall is situated inside what looks like a shipbuilder's warehouse. There is also a counter-service food court (The Riverside Mill), which serves breakfast, lunch, and dinner. Other amenities include stores, an arcade, and playgrounds.

Riverside quick facts and tips

Riverside offers 2,048 rooms.

Each room is approximately 315 square feet.

Rates range from $139 for a standard room in Value Season to $215 for a preferred room in Holiday Season.

The rooms in Alligator Bayou offer a trundle bed and can accommodate five (six with an infant).

The buildings:

The buildings closest to the main building in Alligator Bayou are #14, #15, and #18.

The buildings closest to the main building in Magnolia Bend are Oak Manor and Magnolia Terrace.

More tips:

• One of the downsides to the Alligator Bayou buildings is that there aren't any elevators. On the other hand, the rooms can come with a trundle bed, which allows five people (six with an infant) to sleep in comfort — a boon for families.

• There are four bus stops scattered around Port Orleans–Riverside, so the walk to a bus stop takes no more than five minutes from anywhere in the resort.

• Don't get the preferred rooms unless you want a river view. Remember, a preferred room is at least $15 extra per night.

Fort Wilderness Campground

(2006 Rates: $39 to $92 for campsites, $239 to $349 for cabins)

Camping is an economical option for anyone with a tent, camper, or full-sized RV. Fort Wilderness Campground opened in 1971, just one month after the Magic Kingdom. It spreads out over 700 acres and offers a wealth of outdoor activities along with its campsites and cabins. Guests can bring their own tents, campers, and RVs or rent a cabin that sleeps six in a fair amount of luxury.

Laundry facilities are available in most areas. The WDW transportation system (free to guests) serves Fort Wilderness with both bus and water launch service.

Quick facts and tips

Fort Wilderness has 788 campsites and 407 cabins.

Campsite rates for 2006: $39 for a partial hookup site in Value Season to $92 for a full hookup site in Holiday Season, with non-preferred full hookup sites starting at $44 in Value Season.

Cabin rates for 2006: $239 in Value Season to $349 in Holiday Season.

Campsites sleep ten; cabins sleep six.

All guests get full WDW resort guest privileges.

Babysitting and child-care services are available.

Pets are welcome in some full hookup sites for an extra charge of $5 per night. Inquire for details.

Campsites

All campsites sleep 10 and come with an RV pad, picnic table, trash can, charcoal grill, water, and electricity. Partial hookup sites are the cheapest and come with water and electricity. These sites are only available in non-preferred locations (not close to comfort stations or transportation). Full hookup sites (695 of the campground's 788 sites) cost an additional $5 to $12 a night, but include sewer. The preferred full hookup sites include cable TV as well as sewer and cost $4 to $9 per night more than the non-preferred full hookup sites. Preferred sites are also closer to WDW transportation, restaurants, and comfort stations (restrooms, showers, laundry, and ice).

Cabins

Cabins are air-conditioned, sleep six, and are equipped with most of the amenities of a Moderate Resort, plus a few that are available only here. You'll find:

Fully equipped kitchen.

Bedroom that sleeps four (in a double and bunk bed).

Living area (with a pull-down bed that sleeps two).

Dining table that seats six.

Patio deck, picnic table, and charcoal grill.

Phones with voicemail, irons, ironing boards, coffee makers, hair dryers, cable TVs, and VCRs in each room.

In-room safes.

A fold-away crib.

Daily housekeeping.

Fort Wilderness offers many activities and recreation facilities that the whole family will enjoy. There are two pools, a petting zoo, hiking and nature trails, a convenience store, restaurants, and, for an extra fee, horseback riding. You can dine at the Trail's End restaurant, the *Hoop-Dee-Doo Musical Revue*, and Mickey's Backyard BBQ. The Trails End serves an all-you-can-eat buffet at breakfast, lunch, and dinner. The *Hoop-Dee-Doo Musical Revue* (all-you-can-eat dinner show) and Mickey's Backyard BBQ (all-you-can-eat character picnic with country western entertainment) are reservations-only affairs. There is also a counter-service establishment called Crockett's Tavern that offers drinks and light snacks.

> *Tip:* The *Hoop-Dee-Doo Musical Revue* is one of Disney World's most popular entertainments. Performed three times a night, it costs $50 for adults and $25 for kids three to nine. You can make reservations for it up to two years in advance. If your heart's set on seeing it, be sure to book as soon as you have definite dates for your visit.

As a cost-saving strategy, staying at Fort Wilderness can pay off big for your family. Even though it is a campground, it is considered a Disney Resort and it comes with all the privileges of the other WDW resorts. You can charge purchases to your site and have the items delivered to the campground office. You get free WDW transportation, free parking at the parks, and can take advantage of Disney's Extra Magic Hours (see *Chapter Six*). If you fly into Orlando, you can also take advantage of Disney's Magic Express airport pick-up and delivery service (see *Chapter Two*).

Extra Onsite Hotel Tips from "Disney on a Dime"

Gotta have a cooler or fridge. Having a cooling device in your hotel room is imperative for saving on soda and water. You can save a couple of hundred dollars or more during your vacation by supplying your own drinks instead of buying them from Disney and convenience stores (see *Chapter Three*). That makes the extra $10 a night ($10.60 with sales tax) the Value Resorts charge for an in-room refrigerator one of the biggest downsides to staying in them. Before you decide whether to cough up, consider your options:

• The Moderate Resorts provide refrigerators free of charge. Depending on the season, the size of your family, and what discounts are available, you might find the free fridge just enough of a savings to swing your decision to a Moderate Resort room.

• Paying the $10 per night to have a fridge in your Value Resort room could be a good option if it is your only option. If you flew in, could not bring a cooler, and are only staying a couple of nights, renting a refrigerator might save you money. As an overall strategy, however, we advise against it. The $10 a night can add up quickly over the span of your visit. If you stay a week, that's $70 you'll never see again. Yet a family could easily spend much more than that if they have to buy water and soft drinks in the parks.

Before you pay that extra fee, consider these alternatives:

  • If you are driving, bring your own compact fridge ($60), plug-in cooler ($65), or regular cooler ($5-$20).

  • If you fly in, or don't have room for a cooler in your car, stop at the grocery store when you reach Orlando and buy a cheap foam cooler ($2). Throw it away when you check out. Remember, ice is free! Use a cooler and get all the ice you could possibly want from your resort hotel ice machine.

$$aver Tip: You can also buy and pack a collapsible, soft-sided cooler. These are very inexpensive and very efficient. We find that some soft-sided coolers work even better than traditional coolers.

Many economy hotels offsite come with a free fridge and microwave. These appliances come in handy for even the most basic food preparation. If you will need either or both during your stay, factor in the extra cost you will incur by choosing to stay on property.

Don't waste time and money on laundry. You didn't come all the way to Walt Disney World to spend your time washing clothes. Unless you are staying for an extended period of time, pack enough clothes for your whole stay and do laundry only in emergencies. And if you have to do it, at least supply your own detergent.

In the swim. The official policy at WDW is that guests can only use the pool(s) at their own resort, but it is not unusual to see guests of one resort trying a pool at another.

SAVE ON LODGING

Part 3: Save More by Staying Offsite

It is amazing how much you can save in hotel expenses by staying offsite. It is not only far cheaper in most cases than staying on Disney property, but also offers a number of other benefits. There are more choices of places to stay and types of rooms to stay in. If you like to travel with your pet, Fido or Fluffy can stay in the room with you at many offsite hotels (depending on their size and usually for an additional charge). Disney does not allow pets in its resort rooms. You must board them at a Disney kennel whatever their size. Staying offsite also offers a little "sanity" break for those who aren't Disney fanatics. Let's face it, going to Walt Disney World is sometimes a sacrifice that parents and loved ones make for the rest of the group. Watching cartoons, talking to people in costumes, and riding Dumbo all day can be a little much for some. Staying offsite gives those individuals the break they need to keep smiling.

In this chapter, we will discuss the chief pros and cons of staying offsite and then give you all the tips you need to find that special offsite place to spend your vacation. We'll also list some hotels in the Disney World area that offer good value for your money.

Benefits of Staying Offsite

Hard as it may be for some to believe, there are some benefits to staying offsite. Whether they outweigh the drawbacks is for you to decide.

More for Less

Not only are hotels offsite cheaper, but also many of them have bigger rooms than the WDW hotels offer, and a number come with extras like kitchenettes.

Some even offer full suites with extra bedrooms for less than you would pay to stay at a Value Resort on Disney property. In 2004, for example, we paid just $32 per night for a suite during the Value Season. We would have had to pay $77 for a single room in a WDW Value Resort. Because we number more than four, however, our family would have needed two rooms at a cost of $154 a night.

Room for the whole family

Disney's Value Resorts can accommodate only four people per room (five if one is an infant). Unfortunately, this doesn't fit a lot of families. If you are one of them and you want to stay in a hotel onsite, you will generally have two choices: take two rooms or pay even more for a luxury or home-away-from-home suite (see *Chapters Six* and *Seven*). In contrast, many offsite hotels can accommodate six or more guests in the same room. Some offer specialized multi-room "Kid Suites" or "Family Suites" that have special rooms and amenities for the kids, complete with bunk beds, a video game player, and a TV. The Kid Suites generally cost a little more than the average single room, but for around $50 to $120 a night total, they can be cheaper than booking two separate rooms at Disney.

Free breakfast

Always look for the "free breakfast." Most offsite hotels offer a free continental breakfast with your stay. Be sure to ask what the breakfast includes. An extra $5 a night could be money well spent for a hotel that offers more breakfast options than doughnuts and juice. Also, ask if they have a dining room. Many places have converted a motel room or a tiny corner of the lobby into a breakfast area so they can say that they offer a free breakfast. It's far nicer to stay in a place that has a separate dining room with plenty of tables and chairs for its breakfasting guests.

A free breakfast can save your family or group a lot of money over the course of your vacation. A family of four can easily spend $15 to $20 on breakfast outside the park and well over $40 inside the park. Twenty dollars a day over a seven-day stay is $140 that you can save or put to use elsewhere.

> *$$aver Tip:* Many hotels let you get your breakfast and take it back to the room to eat. Take advantage of fruit and snacks that can be eaten later on in the day to help with the overall food budget. Just don't get greedy. One piece per person is a good rule of thumb.

"Kids Eat Free" offers

Some hotels advertise, "Kids eat free." This is a good deal if you already planned on eating meals at the hotel restaurant. But read the fine print and ask questions when extended this offer. Most of the time, kids eat free only if their parents buy a meal, and the deal may be restricted to one child per adult. If you have four children, only two children will eat for free. If you have small children and all they eat are a bowl of dry cereal and a doughnut, you won't save a lot of money.

> *Bottom line:* "Kids eat free" can save you money if you plan to eat out. If you don't plan to eat out, look for the "free breakfast" offered to all hotel guests instead.

The comforts of home

An in-room fridge and microwave are great options. Look for them. A lot of hotels in the Orlando area offer these amenities for free. With a refrigerator, you can keep all your perishable food cold. You can also freeze the water bottles, yogurt containers, and juice bottles you want to take into the parks with you. Freeze such items overnight, and then use them instead of ice in your cooler the next day. You'll be able to pack more into the cooler and the items will stay cold throughout the day.

With a microwave, you can cook hot meals in the room. Ravioli, Easy Mac, oatmeal, Hot Pockets®, Pizza Rolls, personal frozen pizzas, and popcorn are all favorites that can substitute for a meal. Although it is tough (and not very fairytale-like) to eat such foods all the time, they can take the place of a lunch or dinner here and there.

> *$$aver Tip:* Offsite hotel rooms may even have kitchenettes. This can really save you money during your vacation by making any extra expense for food almost nonexistent. After all, you would have cooked and eaten at home, right? With a kitchenette in your room, you can make your regular meals and save money by not eating out or buying packaged foods.

You can stay with a "friend"

It is sometimes a gamble to stay at an unknown hotel. If you aren't familiar with its standards and policies, you could get a bad deal. However, if you have a favorite chain, one you trust and have a relationship with, you can feel confident booking there. You may be able to save some money, too. Many chains offer free nights, memberships, and other discounts to their loyal customers. If you've earned any free nights, you could apply them to your vacation trip and reduce your overall budget needs. Consider this when weighing the costs.

Just minutes away

Many offsite hotels are within five miles of Disney property, and most of the rest are within ten miles. Your drive (or shuttle) to the parks will add a little time to your commute, but it isn't that bad. If you were to stay at a Value Resort on Disney property, you wouldn't be much closer than if you stayed offsite within five miles of WDW. You would need to stay at a Deluxe or Moderate Disney Resort to have really close access to the parks. We don't recommend this if saving money is your goal.

Free shuttle to the parks

Many offsite hotels offer a free shuttle to and from the WDW parks. This service allows you to stay offsite without having to a rent a car or hire a taxi. However, the service is not guaranteed and comes with some major built-in drawbacks. (See "Drawbacks to Staying Offsite," below.)

At-your-door parking

If you have a car, a big advantage of staying at most offsite hotels is that you can drive right up to the door of your room. If you can't drive right to your door, you can probably get a lot closer than you could if you were staying on Disney property. At most Disney hotels there is quite a distance between you and the parking lot. This is great in terms of letting you lose yourself in the Disney atmosphere, but it is not so great when you want to leave or return to your hotel quickly.

The timesaving advantage of at-the-door parking could compensate for the extra time it will take you to drive to and from an offsite hotel. And parking at the door is a big advantage when loading and unloading your vehicle: packing and unpacking a family trip to Disney World is no small chore.

Discounts for non-Disney attractions

Many offsite hotels offer discounts to Universal, SeaWorld, and other area attractions. Since Disney and Universal are fierce competitors, you will never see these discount offers while staying on Disney property. If you aren't a dedicated Disney fan, or you simply want to see more of the Orlando area during your visit, the discounts and combo packages offered by offsite hotels can help you save money. You'll also be closer to the non-Disney attractions.

Drawbacks to Staying Offsite

Interruption of the Disney magic

Most die-hard resort fans would argue that by staying offsite you tend to lose a little bit of that Disney feeling. It is true that many of the offsite hotels lack the glamour and Imagineering that the resort hotels have, but we don't feel that this is a vacation killer. Staying onsite let's you immerse yourself in the Disney spirit, but it isn't necessary for having a great time and enjoying everything.

No quality guarantees

When you stay onsite, you are guaranteed cleanliness and professionalism at every level of accommodations. There are no such guarantees offsite. The condition of the facilities, cleanliness, customer service, amenities, and conduct of the staff can — and do — vary from hotel chain to hotel chain and among the hotels within a chain. Thus, you might find three hotels in the area around Walt Disney World that belong to the same chain but have different owners and offer very different levels of quality and service.

Most hotels around Walt Disney World are reputable and offer excellent facilities. (We describe a few of them below.) There are some, however, that have very poor facilities and could care less that you've come to enjoy a great Disney experience. Therefore, it is important to do your homework and find out exactly what an offsite hotel offers before you book it. Don't rely on the hotel's star rating. It is very hard to gauge just how good a hotel is from that rating. A 2-star hotel might be barely above the 1-star level or almost worthy of a full three stars. Needless to say, there is a big difference between the two.

Use third-party web sites such as Hotels.com and Travelocity.com to get a better fix on the places you're considering. Both offer hotel ratings and feedback from guests who have stayed there. Read them carefully. Also consult with your travel agent if you have one.

Farther to the Parks

There can be a significant amount of extra time expended — some would say, wasted — when you stay offsite. A quick retreat to an offsite hotel for a rest or meal can take 30 minutes to an hour longer than if you were staying onsite. This might or might not feel like a significant waste of time to you. It depends on your needs, wants, and expectations. If you value money over time, it really doesn't matter.

Extra gas expense

Offsite lodging can be ten miles or more away from the parks. This might not seem like a lot of miles, but they can add up over the course of your vacation. For example, if you stay 10 miles from WDW, you will drive at least 20 miles a day just going to and from the parks. If you plan on going back to your lodging for a mid-day break, you'll pile on at least 40 miles a day. That's 280 miles if you stay a week. And that's minimum. It doesn't include trips to the grocery store or driving from park to park.

Calculate the extra gas expense based on your vehicle's gas consumption. If staying in an offsite hotel is only $15 less per night than staying in one of Disney's Value Resorts, it might be a better call to stay onsite, park your car, and use WDW transportation.

Problematic shuttle service

Many offsite hotels offer a shuttle service to and from the WDW parks. But the service is not what most people picture when they think of a shuttle. Hotels in other cities that offer shuttle service to, say downtown or the mall, have their own vans that take their guests (and only their guests) to the particular destination. Most offsite hotels in the Orlando do not have their own shuttle vans. They subscribe to a service that is shared by as many as 20 hotels. As a result, the service is impersonal and the shuttles tend to become very crowded very quickly. If your hotel is one of the last stops, you might have a hard time getting on and could be stuck having to call a taxi.

To make matters worse, the shuttle schedules can be extremely limited. That means you will not have a lot of freedom to come and go from the parks during the day. Some bus routes, in fact, schedule only one pickup in the morning and one return in the afternoon. If the pickup schedule does not match your schedule, you're stuck.

Worst of all, the hotels do not guarantee the service. It is merely an option they make available to their guests. If the bus breaks down, it's not their problem. If there is not enough room to get on, it's not their problem. If you miss the scheduled pickup or return, it's not their problem. They have no commitment to transporting their guests to and from WDW.

In contrast, the transportation WDW provides for its onsite guests runs every 15 to 30 minutes and is very reliable. Disney owns and operates every bus, boat, and monorail in the fleet; so the transportation measures up to guests' expectations.

If you are going to rely on offsite shuttle service during your trip, be sure to ask lots of questions before booking with a particular hotel. Find out what kind of shuttle service it offers, how many daily round-trips the shuttle makes, and the shuttle's schedule. Also try to pin down what the hotel's commitment is to you should something go wrong with the service.

You'll pay to park at the theme parks

Theme park guests who stay offsite have to pay $8 per day for parking — unless they have an Annual Pass. Be sure to include this expense in your vacation budget.

If you don't have an Annual Pass, there is a way to dodge the parking fee, but it's quite time consuming. Park free at Downtown Disney and catch a bus to the Resort hotels. Once there, you can board a WDW bus to the parks.

> *Caution:* Be sure to weigh the value of your time and effort against the $8 savings, and bear in mind that while both buses are free now, that could change at any time, so do not rely heavily on this tip.

> *$$aver Tip:* You can sometimes park free at night. During slow periods, the Disney parking attendants seem to disappear after 6:00 p.m. or so. This is a bonus for those staying off-site who just want to catch the fireworks or a nighttime show, because their parking ends up being free. However, you can't count on not paying at night. In busier periods, parking attendants may stay later. Besides, if you have visited a theme park during the day, you've already paid for your day's parking, so it's a moot point. Remember, your parking receipt from one WDW theme park is good in all the others all day long, until closing time.

Parking can be a hassle

You may find it hard to find a parking spot at the theme parks during busy times of the year, and the traffic could make you forget you are on vacation.

Can't pay with a room key

You will need to carry your wallet, or at least cash or credit cards, to the parks because you won't be able to charge purchases with a room key, as Disney resort guests can do. This isn't exactly a hardship, but it is less convenient. Not having to worry about losing cards or cash is a bonus of staying onsite.

No room delivery from the theme parks

WDW guests can have items they buy in the parks delivered right to their rooms. When you stay offsite, you have to tote them back yourself. You don't have to tote them around all day, however, because the theme park shops will deliver your purchases to the security desk at the front of the park, free of charge, for easy pickup on your way out. This service takes a while, however. Therefore, if you buy things late in the day, you'll have to carry them with you.

> *Tip:* Be sure to ask how long it will take for your purchase to be delivered to the front of the park. If it will take longer than you plan on staying, just hold on to it.

You could be shut out of the parks

This doesn't happen often, but it does happen. On extremely busy days, such as Christmas and July Fourth, the theme parks and parking lots can reach capacity early in the day. When that happens, the park gates close, and the only new guests allowed in are Annual Passholders and resort guests who arrive by WDW transportation.

> *Note:* Capacity closures take place in stages. In the earlier stages (before entry is restricted to Annual Passholders and resort guests who arrive by WDW transportation), guests who have bought their tickets in advance are allowed in, while those who planned to buy tickets at the gate are turned away — yet another reason to buy your tickets ahead of time.

Offsite Lodging Options

Hotels and motels aren't your only alternatives when you stay offsite near Walt Disney World. You can choose from a broad range of house and condo rentals, offering an equally broad range of amenities. You can also camp, which is by far the cheapest alternative.

Home Rentals

Many companies and individuals offer home rentals. Most rental homes have three to four bedrooms or more (as many as seven or more) and many have a private enclosed swimming pool at the back of the house. Rentals for a three- or four-bedroom home average $80 to $120 a night, depending on both the time of year and the source of the quote. During Value Season (see *Chapter One*), homes have been known to rent for as little as $50 a night.

This is a great option for a big family and for groups of families or friends. Say you have two families that total ten people. Everyone could fit into a four-bedroom house, which would typically run you around $600 to $800 a week. If you had to get hotel rooms, you would pay much more. Even if you found three hotel rooms for $50 a night ($150 a night x 7 nights), it would cost $1,050 for the week. By renting a house together, you'd save at least $250 and you'd get a lot more — a full kitchen, dining room, living room, and quite possibly, a private pool!

> *$$aver Tip:* Don't forget the benefits of having a full kitchen. You can save big on food because it gives you the option of preparing some or all meals at the house.

Cut your home-rental costs in half

If you rent a home through a management company, you will pay $1,200 to $2,000 a week minimum. Rent directly from the owner, and you can cut that cost in half. Most rental-home owners have an agreement with the management companies that handle their properties that allows them (the owners) to rent the house out themselves. When owners do this, they pay their management company a flat fee.

Typically, an owner will rent out the exact same home, with the exact same cleaning and management commitment, for half the price that you'd pay if you rented through the management company. The owner is happy because he or she typically pockets more money; you are happy because you saved 50 percent or more, and the management company still gets paid for its services.

You can find rental-home owners on eBay or through a personal web site by searching for "Orlando villas" or "Orlando rental homes." We recommend the former because everything is locked into the owners' eBay ID. If you have any trouble, you have a venue in which to seek recourse or to leave feedback. Search eBay for rentals with the right options, right location (we recommend something around five miles from Disney World), and right price for you. If you find what you want, but don't see the dates that you need, email the owners. Often, they can accommodate you on the dates you want; if not, they may have another house they can offer you.

We have rented numerous homes via eBay over the years and have never been disappointed. The management company and cleaning services always gave us their best treatment, and all of the homes have been spacious, up to date, and very well appointed. We highly recommend this option.

> *$$aver Tip:* You'll find many specials on eBay for weeks in the Value Seasons. This can also be a good source for last-minute accommodations. If there are several homes available for the following week, the landlords will probably be more flexible on price.

Condo Rentals

Rent a condo instead of a house or hotel room. This could save you hundreds of dollars if you have a large family or are going with a big group. Condos and town houses are much cheaper than single-family houses and are much bigger and sometimes cheaper than a hotel room. There are several timeshare establishments around WDW and openings are very common. Check eBay for deals on condos. You will be able to find two- and three-bedroom units for as little as $300 a week in Value Season. For this price, why even think about staying in a hotel?

RV Camping

Camping isn't for everyone, but if it's for you, you can save big bucks on lodging by staying in your RV or travel trailer. There are plenty of campsites near WDW.

Don't have an RV or camper? Find friends or relatives who own one and approach them about renting it. Most of the time their vehicle is probably sitting in storage or in the backyard collecting dust. Offer them $15 to $20 a day to rent it for your trip. This could be a win-win situation: you get a cheap place to stay and they receive money they would have never seen.

> *Warning:* You can rent a travel trailer or a motor home from dealers and others who specialize in RVs. This is *not* a money saver. In fact, it is very expensive. Most travel trailers rent for around $50 to $75 a day, plus whatever charges you may incur for extra mileage and gas. Motor homes can run you $65 to $200 a

day, again plus any mileage fees the dealer accesses and gas. And that's without the cost of the campsite.

The two KOA campgrounds nearest Walt Disney World are listed below.

Finding the Right Place for You

Orlando has such a wealth of places to stay that it can be hard to pinpoint the one that's right for you. We'll offer a few suggestions for hotels later in this chapter, but if you know (or know of) a travel agent who specializes in the Orlando area, you may want to start there. You can also get leads on desirable places to stay, plus area maps, special offers, and free vacation planning kits from the Orlando and Kissimmee Convention and Visitors Bureaus. You'll find them at www.orlandoinfo.com and www.floridakiss.com. Both are great sources of free information that can also point you to money-saving deals. An Orlando-area guidebook can come in handy, too. Besides their lodging tips, the guidebooks' maps can help you sort out locations in relation to Walt Disney World. Whatever your starting point, you'll probably end up doing most of your research on the Web. So here are a number of sites to get you started:

Orlando Area Web Sites

A number of web sites list most of the hotels around Walt Disney World. Most sites can handle your reservations online or over the phone. We particularly like www.disneyvacationguide.com. Use the web sites to check prices, accommodations, ratings, and feedback from guests. After you have a good feel for what you want, call the hotel directly to see if they can offer you a better deal. If you can make a deal with the hotel, it could save you from paying fees that an outside service may tack on. Many hotels, however, refer you to the company that handles their bookings.

Note: www.DISboards.com has a series of message boards devoted to Disney, one of which covers offsite hotels.

Travel Web Sites

Travel web sites let you research hotels, and sometimes other lodging options, and book them online, usually for a modest fee. However, be aware that if you are looking for accommodations for more than four people, these sites will be of limited help. Most sites that book hotel rooms, do not allow you to book a room for more than four people, or even to enter a search for a room that will accommodate more than four. This hampers your ability to search for suites and larger rooms. To find them, search for rooms for four people and then screen the hotels that come up. Look for the word "suite" in the hotel's name and then investigate what it offers. You may have to contact them directly in order to get the special room that you need.

The following are some of the major travel web sites, along with a brief description of what they offer and some advice on using them to best advantage:

www.priceline.com Priceline allows you to name your price for lodging. You can choose among 2-, 3-, and 4-star hotels. If you are looking to save the most money, choose a 2- or 3-star rating. People have been known to get 2-star hotel rooms on Priceline for as little as $20 a night. If you are looking to get more upscale accommodations at a great price, go for the 4-star rating.

$$aver Tip: The 2-star category is your best bet if you are looking for a hotel that offers a free breakfast. Many (not all) 3-star hotels have their own restaurant onsite and do not offer free continental breakfasts.

The biggest problem with using the name-your-price option on Priceline is that you do not get to choose your hotel; Priceline chooses it for you. You also cannot shop around for the best deal. If your offer is accepted you are billed immediately. If that's a concern, you may want to select a hotel for which Priceline posts rates (instead of naming a price and taking what you get). This may cost you a little more, but you'll know where you're staying before you book it. Priceline charges a booking fee.

$$aver Tip: Before using Priceline, try www.biddingfortravel.com. It has an excellent Priceline tutorial and message boards where people post their winning bids. Check it out. It will help ensure that you don't overbid and pay more than you have to.

www.travelocity.com In our experience, Travelocity has some of the best deals on airfare and offsite hotels, typically a couple of dollars to several hundred dollars cheaper than you'll find on other sites. You can often cut the costs even more by buying your airfare and hotel "as a package."

www.hotels.com Typically this site does not offer the best prices, but it can help you see what's out there. Use it as a research tool.

www.expedia.com Expedia not only lets you see what's out there but also offers some great deals (including good Disney packages). As always before booking through a third party, try to contact the hotel directly to see if you can get a better deal on your own.

www.skyauction.com This site can lead you to cheap condo rentals and free timeshare stays. SkyAuction.com lets you bid on air tickets and lodging. You can read about the hotel, condo, etc. before placing your bid, and some bids start at $1. You might be able to land a week in a condo for $10 — or $205 after the cleaning fee the site imposes. Still that's seven nights for just $205, not a bad price to pay.

If you are interested staying for just two to three nights and don't mind listening to a 90- to 120-minute sales presentation, you may be able to find one through SkyAuction for free — complete with a couple of one-day passes to a WDW theme park. It's not for us, but if it's for you, it could be a very good deal.

Other sites you may want to check include: www.touristflorida.com/hotels and www.usahotelguide.com. Both offer a wide variety of area hotels.

Hotel-Chain Web Sites

If you have a favorite hotel chain, check its web site. Some chains save their best (or only) deals for their web sites. The chain's web site may also be the only place that the hotel will allow you to book reservations online.

Visit www.hotelstravel.com/chains.html or www.hotel-chains-online.com for a complete list of all of the major hotel chain web sites.

Some Affordable Offsite Hotels

Offsite hotels vary in size, class, cost, and condition. The list below includes a few that we consider a good value. We have focused on:

> • Hotels that offer suites ($50 to $90 a night, depending on season),
>
> • Affordable Downtown Disney hotels ($65 to $120), and
>
> • Moderate chain hotels ($30 to $75; you can use frequent lodger points at many of these.)

All of our choices are 3-star hotels, many of which offer free breakfast, that can be booked for under $100 a night in most seasons. In Value Season, the prices can drop extremely low, to $30 a night or just slightly higher at some of these facilities. Tax (around 13%) is additional.

You can find many cheaper hotels than the ones we list, but due to the relative view of what a "decent" or "nice" hotel is, we left them out. Even the ones listed below will not satisfy everybody. Some people will come away from a given hotel feeling that the rooms were clean, the customer service timely, and the décor pleasing. The next person to stay there might leave with the opposite impression, either because they arrived with different expectations or because they had an unpleasant experience of some kind during their stay.

Please, remember to fully investigate any hotel that interests you. Look at the photos, read the feedback from former guests, and weigh your options. Our listing is only a guide, not a full recommendation. Only you can decide what is most likely to fulfill your expectations.

> *Note:* Many of the hotels that we selected have earned Disney's "Good Neighbor Hotel" designation. This gives the hotel a little bit more creditability than the others, because it indicates that they have demonstrated quality in their accommodations, reliability, and service. It also means they can sell WDW admission tickets.

> *Note, too:* All the hotels have pools and a number of them have kiddie pools as well. This is, after all, Florida.

A Word about Suite Hotels

Many offsite hotels offer their guests a little bit more than the standard box. These hotels have one-bedroom suites, two-bedroom suites, or a special room called a kid's suite. They can be a good option for families that don't fit into a room for four. They are also a good option for groups. Here are the typical suite options you'll find:

• One-bedroom suites typically have either a separate bedroom, or a larger room that is partially divided off. These commonly have a living area with a couch and may come with a full kitchen or kitchenette.

• A two-bedroom suite is extra nice for families; some can sleep up to eight. But be sure to compare their cost to what you would pay for two adjacent hotel rooms

• A kid's suite offers the kids some space of their own, within a larger room. The kid's area will normally have a set of bunk beds, a separate TV, and games such as Nintendo. As always, look over your options and make a decision based on your needs and your pocketbook. And bear in mind that a hotel does not have to have the word "suite" in its name to offer its guests suite options.

Hotels in Kissimmee

MainStay Suites Maingate

4786 West Irlo Bronson Memorial Highway (US 192)
Kissimmee, FL 34746
407-396-2056
www.choicehotels.com

General Information:

5 Miles to Disney Property
Rating: ***
Room Capacity: 6
Free Breakfast: Yes
Shuttle Service to WDW: Yes
Full Kitchen: Yes
Pets Welcome: Yes (for $10 per night; must be 25 lb. or under)

Room Amenities:

Living Area with Sofa Bed
Phone
TV
Radio Alarm Clock
Coffee Maker
Iron
Ironing Board
Refrigerator
Microwave
Dishwasher
Pots and Pans

Property Amenities:

Free Newspaper
Coin Laundry
Fitness Room
Spa
Basketball
Business Center
Sandy Beach
Picnic Area
Playground

Quality Suites Maingate East

5876 West Irlo Bronson Memorial Highway (US 192)
Kissimmee, FL 34746
407-396-8040
www.choicehotels.com

General Information:

1.7 Miles to Disney Property
Walt Disney World Good Neighbor Hotel
Rating: ***
Room Capacity: 6 to 10
Free Breakfast: Yes
Shuttle Service to WDW: Yes
Full Kitchen: Yes
Pets Welcome: Yes (for $10-$15 per night if pet room available)

Room Amenities:

Living Area with Sofa Bed
2 Phones
2 TVs
High-Speed Internet
Radio Alarm Clock
Coffee Maker
Iron
Ironing Board
Refrigerator
Microwave
Dishes

Property Amenities:

Coin Laundry
Spa
Poolside Bar
Video Arcade
Business Center
Car Rental
Gift Shop
Free Happy Hour

Seralago Hotel and Suites Maingate East

(formerly known as Holiday Inn Hotel and Suites Maingate East)

5678 Irlo Bronson Memorial Highway (US 192)

Kissimmee, FL 34746

407-396-4488

www.orlando-family-fun-hotel.com

General Information:

3 Miles to Disney Property

Walt Disney World Good Neighbor Hotel

Rating: ***

Room Capacity: 5 to 8

Free Breakfast: No (Kids Eat Free at Restaurant)

Shuttle Service to WDW: Yes

Full Kitchen: Yes

Pets Welcome: Yes (for $25 for length of stay; must be 30 lb. or
under)

$$aver Tip: Call or go to their web site for special rates and deals (Example: Stay two nights and get the third free). Deals are constantly on offer, but you have to ask to get them.

Room Amenities:

Kid's Suites with Bunk Beds Available

Living Area with Sofa Bed

Phones

2 TVs

Radio Alarm Clock

Coffee Maker

Iron

Refrigerator

Microwave

Property Amenities:

Coin Laundry	Tennis
Fitness Room	2 Playgrounds
2 Pools and 2 Spas	General Store
Basketball	Pool Bar
Video Arcade	Food Court
Business Center	Restaurant

Free Nightly Movies in Property's Movie Theatre

Hotels in Downtown Disney

Downtown Disney has several hotels that are looked on by Disney as almost their own. This is where many upscale chain hotels have been allowed to set up shop and cater to travelers who want to stay in familiar surroundings. Hotels in this area have very quick access not only to Downtown Disney, but also to the Disney theme parks. We have listed two that are relatively easy on the wallet, but there are several more in the Downtown Disney area that might work for you. If you have points built up with Hilton, Marriott, or Doubletree, check out their hotels for possible savings.

Best Western Lake Buena Vista Resort Hotel

2000 Hotel Plaza Boulevard
Lake Buena Vista, FL 32830
800-348-3765
407-828-2424
www.bestwestern.com

General Information:

1 Mile to Disney Property, 0.5 Miles to Downtown Disney
Walt Disney World Good Neighbor Hotel
Rating: ***
Room Capacity: 4
Free Breakfast: No
Shuttle Service to WDW: Yes
Full Kitchen: No
Pets Welcome: No

Room Amenities:

Private Balcony
Phone
TV
Radio Alarm Clock
Coffee Maker
Iron
Ironing board

Property Amenities:

Coin Laundry	Business Center
Fitness Room	Restaurant
Playground	

Grosvenor Resort

1850 Hotel Plaza Boulevard
Lake Buena Vista, FL 32830
800-624-4109
407-828-4444
www.grosvenorresort.com

General Information:

1 Mile to Disney Property, 0.5 Miles to Downtown Disney
Walt Disney World Good Neighbor Hotel
Rating: ***
Room Capacity: 4+
Free Breakfast: No
Shuttle Service to WDW: Yes
Full Kitchen: No
Pets Welcome: No

Room Amenities:

Kid's Suites available
Phone
TV
Internet
Radio Alarm Clock
Coffee Maker
Iron
Ironing Board

Property Amenities:

Disney Character Breakfast Is Offered
Aquatic Center
Fitness Room
Game Room
Business Center
Restaurant
Rental Car Company

Moderate Chain Hotels

These are mid-range hotels in terms of both price and amenities. Most aren't too fancy, but at the same time they aren't no-name establishments. All but one are 3-star hotels, and offer nice amenities and good service.

Country Inn & Suites

12191 South Apopka Vineland Road
Lake Buena Vista, FL 32830
407-239-1115
www.countryinns.com

General Information:

1 Mile to Disney Property
Rating: ***
Room Capacity: 4
Free Breakfast: Yes
Shuttle Service to WDW: Yes
Full Kitchen: No
Pets Welcome: No

Room Amenities:

Kid's Suites Available
Phone
TV
Radio Alarm Clock
Coffee Maker
Iron
Ironing Board
Refrigerator
Microwave

Property Amenities:

Free Local Calls
Free Newspaper
Coin Laundry
Fitness Room
Business Center
High-Speed Internet
Gift Shop

Clarion Hotel Maingate

7675 West Irlo Bronson Highway (US 1§
Kissimmee, FL 34747-8201
407-396-4000
www.choicehotels.com

G

General Information:

1.3 Miles to Disney Property
Walt Disney World Good Neighbor Hotel
Rating: ***
Room Capacity: 4
Free Breakfast: No (Kids Eat Free)
Shuttle to Disney: Yes
Full Kitchen: No
Pets Welcome: No

Room Amenities:

Phone
TV
Wi-Fi Internet Access (high-speed also available)
Radio Alarm Clock
Coffee Maker
Hair Dryer
Iron
Ironing Board

Property Amenities:

Fitness Room
Dining Room
Kids' Activities
Meeting Rooms
Dry Cleaning Onsite
Restaurant

Quality Inn Maingate West

7785 West Irlo Bronson Highway (US 192)
Kissimmee, FL 34747
407-396-1828
www.choicehotels.com

eneral Information:

1.5 Miles to Disney Property
Rating: **
Room Capacity: 4
Free Breakfast: Yes
Shuttle to Disney: Yes
Full Kitchen: No
Pets Welcome: No

Room Amenities:

Phone
Cable TV
Data Ports
Radio Alarm Clock
Iron
Ironing Board

Property Amenities:

Restaurant
Guest Laundry Facilities
Free Coffee
Free Local Calls
Safe Deposit Boxes

Radisson Inn Lake Buena Vista

8686 Palm Parkway
Orlando, FL 32836-6434
800-333-3333
407-239-8400
www.radisson.com

General Information:

1 Mile to Disney Property
Walt Disney World Good Neighbor Hotel
Rating: ***
Room Capacity: 4
Free Breakfast: No
Shuttle to Disney: Yes
Full Kitchen: No
Pets Welcome: No

Room Amenities:

Private Balcony
Phone
Cable TV
High-Speed Internet
Coffee Maker
Iron
Ironing Board
Hair Dryer

Property Amenities:

Room Service
Free Newspaper
Fitness Room
Dining Room
Playground
Kids' Activities
Dry Cleaning Onsite
Restaurant

Best Western Lakeside

7769 West Irlo Bronson Memorial Highway (US 192)
Kissimmee, FL 34747
407-396-2222
www.bestwestern.com

General Information

1.8 Miles to Disney Property
Walt Disney World Good Neighbor Hotel
Rating: ***
Room Capacity: 4
Free Breakfast: No (Kids Eat Free; ask when making
    your reservations)
Shuttle to Disney: Yes
Full Kitchen: No
Pets Welcome: No

Room Amenities:

Desk
Telephone with Voicemail
TV
Data Port
Coffee Maker
Iron
Ironing board

Property Amenities:

Free Newspaper
Free Local Calls
Fitness Room
3 Outdoor Heated Pools
2 Children's Pools
Playground
Kids' Activities
Miniature Golf Course
Business Center
Meeting Rooms
2 Restaurants

RV Campsites

There are a number of campgrounds in the Orlando area. We've limited our listings to the two KOA sites nearest Walt Disney World, because KOA is a known quantity. Visit its web site (www.koa.com) for more information and pictures of the facilities.

Kissimmee/Orlando KOA
2644 Happy Camper Place
Kissimmee, FL 34746
800-562-7791

Orlando SW KOA
Frontage Road
Lake Buena Vista, FL 32830
888-562-4712

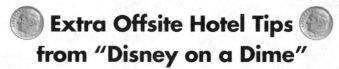

Extra Offsite Hotel Tips from "Disney on a Dime"

Call hotels directly. If you find what looks like a nice hotel on a web site, type its full name and location into www.google.com or another search engine to get its phone number. Calling the hotel directly allows you to ask questions, avoid booking fees, and possibly get a better deal. Remember, always ask for the best deal.

> *$$aver Tip:* You could also ask the hotel to match someone else's offer. This can be a great way to get the best price on the hotel that you want. The market is fairly competitive around Disney World.

Pinpoint taxes and fees. Be aware that tax rates in the Orlando area vary by county and that some counties tack various fees onto hotel bills in addition to the tax. You can't avoid paying them, but you should know what they are. Travelocity, Priceline, and other online travel sites generally charge a booking fee, as do many booking services that handle reservations by phone. Find out what the fee will be before using the service.

Always ask for a complete quote that includes all taxes, county fees, resort fees, hotel add-ons, and any additional services you may want, such as a crib for the baby or Internet access. When you book directly with the hotel, ask for a waiver of any add-ons (for example, surcharges for rooms with data ports or in-room safes), or at least how you can avoid them (perhaps by booking in a different room category). You won't always get the waiver, but you will know the total charge upfront so that there aren't any surprises later.

Note: You'll often have to push the hotel reservationist to give you the total price. Just be patient and stick with it until you are sure you have the total before you make the booking or put down a deposit.

Ask for a discount if staying a week or more. Call the hotel directly and ask if they have a weekly rate or a discount for staying more than a certain number of days. Most web sites and reservation services do not account for multi-day savings. A weekly rate might knock $3 to $10 off the nightly rate. That's a savings of $21 to $70 of your week's stay. Every little bit helps.

Don't worry about waiting to book a room. Unless you are going in Holiday Season, don't worry about waiting until the last minute to book a room offsite. Keep shopping around for the best deal. They tend to be offered when a hotel has a lot of rooms and no guests. If you are the risk-taking type, just show up and look at the marquees outside the hotels. Many times we have booked rooms at a great rate only to find a better rate flashing in the front of the hotel (or across the street) on arrival.

Don't be afraid to renegotiate your rate. If your hotel is offering a better rate now than the one you booked, ask for the better rate. If they refuse because you already have a reservation, ask how much notice is required for cancellation of your reservations. If the cancellation period is only 24 hours, agree to stay one night, cancel the rest of your reservation, and then re-book under the better deal.

$$aver Tip: If they do not want to work with you, threaten (nicely, of course) to go to another hotel. There is plenty of competition in the area, so most hotels will work with you. It is better for them to make some profit off of you than to have you go across the street, especially during Value Season.

Don't fall for the "Kids Stay Free" gimmick. A lot of hotels still boast that "Kids Stay Free!" at their establishments. What hotel still charges for kids under 18? The fact is that not charging for children has become the industry standard. Do not consider this a cost savings when weighing the benefits of one hotel over another.

Be sure you have a cooler or fridge. Having a cooling device in your hotel room is essential for saving on soda and water. You can save a couple of hundred dollars or more on a week's family vacation by supplying your own drinks instead of buying them in the theme parks and convenience stores. So we will repeat here a bit of the advice we offered in the previous chapter:

Choose a place with a refrigerator if at all possible. This should not be difficult when you are staying offsite. But, if for some reason, the place you book does not offer in-room refrigerators:

- Bring your own compact fridge ($60), plug-in cooler ($65), or regular cooler ($5-$20), or

- Stop at the grocery store when you reach Orlando and buy a cheap foam cooler ($2). Get the ice you need from the hotel ice machine. Throw the cooler away when you check out.

There may be a good reason it's cheap. When shopping for an offsite hotel, you have a very good chance of finding a high quality hotel room for a good price. You also have a slight chance of getting a cheap room for a cheap price. If you pay $20 a night for a no-name hotel, don't expect a grand foyer and top-notch service. It could be out of date, dirty, or far from Disney World.

Sometimes it can be better to spend a little bit more for the security of getting a decent place to sleep. If you find a great rate at Bob's Motel, but can stay at the Sleep Inn for $10 more a night, do it. Even chain hotels have their quirks, but at least you have a better idea of what you are getting into.

Getting The Best of Both Worlds:
Enjoy "Extra Magic Hours" Perks & Offsite Prices

Disney's resort guests have the special privilege of enjoying "Extra Magic Hours" in the WDW theme parks — an hour in the morning and up to three hours in the evening when a designated park is closed to the general public and open only to resort guests. With a little creative planning, you can stay offsite and still take advantage of this special perk. Here's how:

Book a campsite at Disney's Fort Wilderness Campground for a night. You won't have to stay there; you'll just have to check in and out. At a cost of around $40 in Value Season, (rising to $72 during Christmas week), a one-night stay will entitle you to all WDW resort guest privileges for two days. These include Extra Magic Hours, free parking at the theme parks, and free use of the Disney transportation system to move from park to park.

> *Note:* You'll still need admission tickets to get into the parks, of course, with a Hopper option if you want to take full advantage of your Magic Hours privilege (see *Chapter Six*).

Why spend the extra bucks? You'll get to experience the parks up to eight hours longer (four hours each day) than other offsite guests. And since the parks will be less crowded at those times, you'll be able to do and see more. An extra plus, if you don't have an Annual Pass, is the free parking you get as a resort guest. You'll recoup $16 of your campsite cost immediately.

To take full advantage of this strategy, we recommend that you check in early (7:30 a.m.) on the first morning of your campsite "stay" and check out early on the second. Your resort-guest benefits extend through midnight of day two. If you pay with a credit card, you won't even have to check out.

> *Note:* We figure it took us about 15 minutes total to use this strategy for a one-night campground "stay."

> *$$aver Tip:* If you want to take advantage of these benefits during your whole stay, you can save money by checking in and out every other day.

- Sample Budget Itineraries

- Food Budgets

- Extra Tips

SAMPLE BUDGETS & MENUS

This chapter is intended to help you prepare a vacation budget. It is very important to consider all aspects of your vacation. Figure how much you can spend and how much things are going to cost, then plan accordingly. Remember the old saying, "Fail to Plan, Plan to Fail?" On a vacation, this can translate into "Fail to Plan, Plan to Spend A Lot of Money." We personally know a lot of people who did not fully plan their vacation budgets and ended up spending a week's allotment in a couple of days. This is very easy to do on any vacation and even easier to do at Walt Disney World, where everything is so very attractive and, all too often, somewhat pricey.

Planning lets you evaluate your needs and the actual cost of tickets, transportation, lodging, food, and souvenirs *before* you are stranded in the parks with a very hungry family. Use the sample budgets and menus in this chapter as guides for developing a budget and eating plans of your own. The samples include only the very basics. For example, every meal is calculated without any purchased beverages and we've allotted only one souvenir per person. Many people will not have to be that conservative with their money, but we wanted to show you the minimal practical costs involved in a Disney World vacation.

> *Caution:* Taxes and fees can add a big chunk of change to your vacation costs. We have not included them here or in our other chapters because they vary depending on where you buy your tickets, food, etc., and where you stay. The rates vary even within Walt Disney World because it straddles two different counties. So the resort tax ranges from 11.5% to 13% and sales tax from 6.5% to 7%. Be sure to allow for taxes and fees in your budget.

159

Look at all of your options, use the tips we offer throughout this book to find ways to save on every aspect of your vacation. Add any extras that are important to you (gotta have that morning latte?). Then make your itinerary and budget for it:

- If you can't imagine a trip to Walt Disney World without a Character Meal, add it in.

- If you just have to have a pair of Mouse Ears for each of the kids, add them in.

- If a vacation isn't complete without a splurge for a bit of luxury, identify just what that is, and add it in.

When you've figured it all out, replace our numbers with your estimated costs for gas, airfare, food, lodging, souvenirs and any extras you want.

Overall planning is not only the best way to save money, but also the best way to ensure that you'll be able to do and see all that is most important to you on your Walt Disney World vacation. Remember, a Disney World vacation is within the reach of almost everyone. You just have to be willing to do what it takes to save up your money and spend it for what matters most to you once you get to Walt Disney World.

About the Sample Budgets

All the budget itineraries in this chapter are based on a family of four, two adults and two children between the ages of three to nine, visiting during Value Season. This obviously won't cover everyone's situation. But it is a good start that makes it easy to compare the costs of various alternatives, such as longer and shorter stays and eating meals in your hotel room versus eating them out. If your children are ten or older, bear in mind that you will have to buy them adult tickets for the theme parks (see *Chapter Four*).

Bear in mind, too, that the prices we quote are generally *before* tax, which will add 6.5% to 7% to food charges and 11% to 13% to lodging.

Budget #1

No Money, But You Just Gotta Go

(2 Days in the Theme Parks)

If you absolutely have to go to Disney World and want to see all of the parks in just two days, a family of four can do that for $630 plus tax and the cost of travel. The trick is to stay offsite in a hotel that offers a free breakfast; eat your other meals in your hotel room, and bring your own snacks and drinks into the parks with you.

If you truly want to take your family to Disney World, this is probably the cheapest way to do it. Plan to stay three nights so that you can spend two full days in the parks, and bid for a cheap hotel on Priceline.com. This isn't the cheapest option on a per-day basis, but it will cost you the least overall. Remember, to add in the cost of travel.

Budget One: 2 Days in the Theme Parks/Offsite Hotel		
Gas/Airfare	Depends on Distance and Size of Vehicle	Varies
Tickets	2-Day Base Tickets (2 adult, 2 child)	$430*
Hotel	3 Nights at Offsite Discount Hotel (as low as $25 a night)	$75
Food	• "Free Breakfast" at Hotel	FREE
	• Lunch & Dinner in Hotel Room (sandwiches/fast food)	$50
	• Bring Own Water & Snacks to Parks (24 bottles of water plus 8 sets of snacks)	$15
Souvenirs	Pre-Buy and Bring with You (Allow one souvenir per person for the trip; $15 per person)	$60
Total		**$630***

*If you wanted to visit all four theme parks during your two-day trip, you could buy Park Hopper options for your base tickets. The additional cost would be $140, for a total of $770 plus tax.

Budget #2
Stay Offsite, Spend a Day in Each Park
(4 Days in the Theme Parks)

For a little bit more than it would cost you to visit the theme parks for two days, your family can go to the parks for four full days. Again stay offsite, this time for five nights, and again plan to eat all your meals in your room. Buy 4-day tickets and bring snacks and drinks into the parks with you. Don't forget to add in the cost of your travel.

Budget Two: 4 Days in the Theme Parks / Stay Offsite

Gas/Airfare	Depends on Distance and Size of Vehicle	Varies
Tickets	4-Day Base Tickets* (2 adult, 2 child)	$667*
Hotel	5 Nights at Offsite Hotel (with fridge and microwave in room; as low as $30 a night)	$150
Food	• Breakfast at Hotel	FREE
	• Lunch & Dinner in Hotel Room (sandwiches, mac & cheese, ravioli, pizza	$75
	• Bring Own Water & Snacks to Parks (48 bottles of water, 16 sets of snacks)	$30
Souvenirs	Pre-buy and Bring with You (Allow one souvenir per person for the trip; $15 per person)	$60
Total		**$982***

*If you wanted to visit more than one theme park per day during your trip, you could buy Park Hopper options for your base tickets. The additional cost would be $140, for a total of $1,121 plus tax.

Budget #3

Stay On Property, Spend a Day in Each Park

(4 Days in the Theme Parks, Room-Only Reservation)

You can stay at a Disney World Value Resort, enjoy the parks for four full days, and have a blast for just a bit over $1,500, including the tax on your hotel and tickets. Stay onsite during Value Season, eat in your hotel room, and bring your own snacks and drinks into the parks with you. Remember to add in the cost of your travel.

Budget Three: 4 Days in the Theme Parks / Stay On Property

Gas/Airfare	Depends on Distance and Size of Vehicle	Varies
Tickets	• 4-Day Base Tickets*	$667
	• Park Hopper Options*	$140*
	(2 adult, 2 child)	
Hotel	5 Nights at Value Resort Onsite (Value Season @ $79 a night +13% Tax)	$446
Food	• Breakfast, Lunch & Dinner (in hotel room; make sandwiches)	$115
	• Bring Own Water and Snacks to Parks (48 bottles of water, 16 sets of snacks)	$30
Souvenirs	Pre-buy and Bring with You (Allow one souvenir per person for the trip; $15 per person)	$60
Total		**$1,458***

*If you want to visit more than one theme park per day during your trip, you will need to buy Park Hopper options for your base tickets. Without these options, your total would be $1,318 before tax.

Food Budgets
for a 5-Day/4-Night Stay

You have lots of options when it comes to eating. They range from eating all your meals in your hotel room (boring but cheap) to eating all your meals out (fairly pricey to sky's the limit). The table below lets you see at a glance how much you might budget for breakfast, lunch, and dinner (13 meals total) for each of six options. Totals are based on feeding a family of two adults and two children younger than ten years of age. The six "menus" that follow are intended to give you an idea of what you could eat for the prices we've quoted in the table below.

Remember, the choice is up to you. If you prefer to eat all your dinners in sit-down restaurants, go for it. Just be sure to budget what you will need to cover the cost. You may even want to budget for a special dinner out for mom and dad one night plus take-out and a babysitter for the kids.

Six Food Budget Options for 13 Meals				
Breakfast	**Lunch/Dinner**	**Total**	**Per Meal**	**Per Pers.**
Stay Offsite with Free Breakfast	Both Eaten in Hotel Room	$71.50	$5.50	$1.38
Stay Offsite with Free Breakfast	Lunch in the Parks Dinner in Hotel Room	$123.04	$9.46	$2.37
Stay Onsite Breakfast in Room	Both Eaten in Hotel Room	$110.90	$8.53	$2.13
Stay Onsite Breakfast in Room	Lunch in Hotel Room Dinner in Parks	$158.84	$12.22	$3.05
Stay Onsite Breakfast at Resort counter restaurants	Both Eaten in Parks at counter restaurants	$260.83	$20.06	$5.02
Stay Onsite Breakfast at Resort counter restaurants	Both Eaten in Park Restaurants (Lunch at sit-down venues) (Dinner at counter venues)	$349.37	$26.87	$6.72

Food Budget Options

The menus that follow are intended to stimulate your thinking, not to lay out an eating plan for your vacation. They offer very little variety and do not allow for individual taste and sophistication. The point is simply to give you a good sense of the dollar consequences of various eating options. Scan them for ideas of what you could prepare and serve (or order and eat) for about the same amounts. Be creative. Consider what your family likes and plan menus that you would eat. Then budget for them. If your family likes sushi and corn dogs, budget for that. If you are vegans, plan and budget for that. Then add or subtract the difference from the overall budget plan. This will help to prevent both under-budgeting what you will need and overspending when shopping.

> *Note:* All menus assume a family of four (two adults and two young children) and are based on a five-night hotel stay and four days spent in the theme parks.

> *Caution:* These menus cover only thirteen meals, three per day for your four days in the theme parks plus breakfast on your departure day. They do not include any other food you will consume on your arrival and departure days or any additional travel day.

> Be sure your total food budget includes the cost of all the meals, snacks, and drinks you will consume while you are on your trip, not just for the days you spend at the parks.

We offer six options. The prices in our "Grocery List" under each option are averages. You might find these items for a bit more or a bit less.

> *#1.* Stay Offsite. Eat all meals in your hotel room, prepared with the aid of an in-room microwave and refrigerator.

> *#2.* Stay Offsite. Eat breakfast and dinner in your room; lunch in the parks.

> *#3.* Stay Onsite. Eat all meals in your hotel room without the aid of a microwave.

> *#4.* Stay Onsite. Eat breakfast and lunch in your hotel room; eat dinner in the parks.

> *#5.* Stay Onsite. Eat all three meals at Walt Disney World counter-service restaurants.

> *#6.* Stay Onsite. Eat breakfast and dinner at counter-service restaurants and lunch at a sit-down restaurant.

Option #1

All Meals Eaten in Your Offsite Hotel Room

• 5 Breakfasts: Free with hotel room
• 4 Lunches: In hotel room
• 4 Dinners: In hotel room

Lunches: Days 1 & 3

Use ham and cheese and peanut butter and jelly to make sandwiches
Share half a full-size bag of chips
Have pudding cups for dessert (1 per person)
Drink bottled water or soft drinks purchased from the grocery store

Lunches: Days 2 & 4

Heat up mac & cheese or ravioli in your in-room microwave
Share fresh fruit (apples, bananas, oranges)
Have cookies for dessert (share from a bag or box)
Drink bottled water or soft drinks purchased from the grocery store

Dinners: Days 1 & 3

Microwave pizza or pizza rolls
Share a salad
Have cookies for dessert (share from a bag or box)
Drink bottled water or soft drinks purchased from the grocery store

Dinners: Days 2 & 4

Microwave Hot Pockets® or TV dinners
Share a salad
Have snack cakes for dessert (1 per person)
Drink bottled water or soft drinks purchased from the grocery store

Option #1 Grocery List

2 packages of sandwich meat	$5.00
1 package of cheese slices	$2.50
1 jar of jelly	$3.00
1 jar of peanut butter	$3.00
2 loaves of bread	$2.00
1 bag of chips	$2.50
2 four-packs of pudding cups	$3.00
1 microwavable mac & cheese (box of 10)	$8.00

8 pieces of fruit	$9.00
1 box of snack cakes	$1.50
4 personal pizzas	$9.00
1 large bag of salad	$5.00
1 package of cookies	$2.00
6 Hot Pockets® (2 for $3.00)	$9.00
32 drinks (generic sodas and juice boxes)	$7.00

Option #1 Total $71.50

$ per meal (÷13)	$5.50 (with free breakfast)
$ per person/meal (÷52)	$1.38 (with free breakfast)

Option #2
Breakfast, Dinner in Offsite Hotel Room
Lunch in Parks

- 5 Breakfasts: Free with hotel room
- 4 Lunches: At counter-service restaurants in the theme parks
- 4 Dinners: In hotel room

Lunch: Day 1. Cosmic Ray's in Magic Kingdom

2 quarter-pound cheeseburgers with fries	$11.38
2 Children's Meals (come with drinks)	$6.98
Adults drink own beverages or order water	
Total	*$18.36 + tax*

Lunch: Day 2. Electric Umbrella in Epcot

2 deli sandwiches with coleslaw	$12.98
2 Children's Meals (come with drinks)	$6.98
Adults drink own beverages or order water	
Total	*$19.96 + tax*

Lunch: Day 3. Toy Story Pizza Planet in Disney–MGM Studios*

2 pepperoni pizzas	$11.58
2 cheese pizzas	$10.98
Drink own beverages or order water	
Total	*$22.56 + tax*

*Consider this lunch a treat for the kids (more expensive per person)

Lunch: Day 4. Tusker House in Disney's Animal Kingdom

1 fried chicken sandwich with fries	$6.99
1 rotisserie chicken with mashed potatoes and vegetable	$7.99
2 Children's Meals (come with drinks)	$6.98
Adults drink own beverages or order water	
Total	*$21.96 + tax*

Dinners: Days 1 & 3

Microwave pizza or pizza rolls
Share a salad
Have cookies for dessert
Drink bottled water or soft drinks purchased from the grocery store

Dinners: Days 2 & 4

Heat up mac & cheese or ravioli in your in-room microwave
Share fresh fruit (apples, bananas, oranges)
Have snack cakes for dessert (4 snack cakes)
Drink bottled water or soft drinks purchased from the grocery store

Option #2 Grocery List

1 microwavable mac & cheese (box of 10)	$8.00
8 pieces of fruit	$9.00
1 box of snack cakes	$1.50
4 personal pizzas	$9.00
1 large bag of salad	$5.00
1 package of cookies	$2.00
26 drinks (generic sodas and juice boxes)	$5.70

Option #2 Totals

Groceries	$40.20
Park meals	$82.84 + tax
Grand total	**$123.04**
$ per meal (÷13)	$9.46 (with free breakfast)
$ per person/meal (÷52)	$2.37 (with free breakfast)

Option #3
All Meals Eaten in Your Onsite Hotel Room

This option is a little extreme, because Disney's Value Resort rooms do not have microwaves and refrigerators. You can get a fridge for an extra $10 a day, but we recommend using a cooler or two if you are trying to keep your eating expenses as low as you can (see "Extra Tips," *Chapter Seven*).

> *Note:* You can access a microwave in the food court, and so we have included hot-meal options in the dinner menus. If you're not comfortable going that route, just replace the microwaveable entrees on the grocery list with more sandwich fixings.

- 5 Breakfasts: In your Value Resort hotel room
- 4 Lunches: In your Value Resort hotel room (or picnic in the parks)
- 4 Dinners: In your Value Resort hotel room (or picnic in the parks)

Breakfast: Days 1 through 5
Choose from these items, or mix and match, to suit your breakfast habits
> Doughnuts
> Orange juice
> Milk
> Cereal
> Fruit
> Health shakes/Instant breakfast shakes
> Bagels

Lunches: Days 1 & 3
> Use ham and cheese and peanut butter and jelly to make sandwiches
> Share half a full-size bag of chips
> Have pudding cups for dessert (1 per person)
> Drink bottled water or soft drinks purchased from the grocery store

Lunches: Days 2 & 4
> Heat up mac & cheese or ravioli in your in-room microwave
> Share fresh fruit (apples, bananas, oranges)
> Have cookies for dessert (share from a box or bag)
> Drink bottled water or soft drinks purchased from the grocery store

Dinners: Days 1 & 3
> Microwave pizza or pizza rolls
> Share a salad

Have cookies for dessert (share from a box or bag)

Drink bottled water or soft drinks purchased from the grocery store

Dinners: Days 2 & 4

Microwave Hot Pockets® or TV dinners

Share a salad

Have snack cakes for dessert (1 per person)

Drink bottled water or soft drinks purchased from the grocery store

Option #3 Grocery List

Doughnuts	$10.00
1 gallon orange juice	$3.50
1 gallon milk	$3.00
Cereal	$3.00
Fruit	$6.00
Health shakes/Instant breakfast shakes (6-pack)	$6.00
Bagels	$3.50
2 packages of sandwich meat*	$5.00
1 package of cheese slices*	$2.50
1 jar of jelly*	$3.00
1 jar of peanut butter*	$3.00
2 loaves of bread*	$2.00
1 bag of chips	$2.50
2 four-packs of pudding cups	$3.00
1 microwavable mac & cheese†	$8.00
8 pieces of fruit	$9.00
1 box of snack cakes	$1.50
4 personal pizzas†	$9.00
1 large bag of salad	$5.00
1 package of cookies	$2.00
6 Hot Pockets® (2 for $3.00)	$9.00
52 drinks (generic sodas and juice boxes)	$11.40

*Get twice as much (or similar item) if you don't plan to fix hot entrée items in the food court microwave.

†Eliminate if you don't plan to fix hot entrée items in the food court microwave.

Option #3 Total $110.90

$ per meal (÷13)	$8.53
$ per person/meal (÷52)	$2.13

Option #4
Breakfast, Lunch in Onsite Hotel Room
Dinner in Parks

• 5 Breakfasts: In hotel room
• 4 Lunches: In hotel room
• 4 Dinners: At counter-service restaurants in the theme parks

Breakfast: Days 1 through 5

Choose from these items, or mix and match, to suit your breakfast habits

Doughnuts
Orange juice
Milk
Cereal
Fruit
Health shakes/Instant breakfast shakes
Bagels

Lunches: Days 1 & 3

Use ham and cheese and peanut butter and jelly to make sandwiches
Share half a full-size bag of chips
Have pudding cups for dessert (4 cups)
Drink bottled water or soft drinks purchased from the grocery store

Lunches: Days 2 & 4

Heat up mac & cheese or ravioli in your in-room microwave
   Note: This option may not suit everybody. Disney does not have
   microwaves in its hotel rooms; so you must use the microwave
   located in the food court. If this is an issue for you, just substitute
   sandwiches or something else that doesn't need to be heated.

Share fresh fruit (apples, bananas, oranges)
Have snack cakes for dessert (4 snack cakes)
Drink bottled water or soft drinks purchased from the grocery store

Dinner: Day 1. Cosmic Ray's in Magic Kingdom

2 quarter-pound cheeseburgers with fries	$11.38
2 Children's Meals (come with drinks)	$6.98
Adults drink own beverages or order water	
Total	*$18.36 + tax*

Dinner: Day 2. Electric Umbrella in Epcot

2 deli sandwiches with coleslaw	$12.98
2 Children's Meals (come with drinks)	$6.98
Adults drink own beverages or order water	
Total	**$19.96 + tax**

Dinner: Day 3. Toy Story Pizza Planet in Disney-MGM Studios*

2 pepperoni pizzas	$11.58
2 cheese pizzas	$10.98
Drink own beverages or order water	
Total	**$22.56 + tax**

*Consider this a treat for the kids (more expensive per person)

Dinner: Day 4: Electric Umbrella in Epcot*

Note: While you will spend the day in Disney's Animal Kingdom, you won't be able to eat dinner at its Tusker House counter-service restaurant because it generally closes too early. Typically the park closes around 5:00 p.m. and most of its restaurants close an hour earlier — even on days that the park is open late to WDW Resort guests for Extra Magic Hours. Snack kiosks and carts will be available if you want to grab a snack or something to drink, but full meals are not served in the park in the evening. The Rain Forest Café, a sit-down restaurant near the park entrance, is open every night until 6:30 p.m. If you plan to spend Extra Magic Hours in the park, you could fill up there first. On days when the park isn't open late, plan on eating counter-service after you leave Animal Kingdom. You could eat at Cosmic Ray's in Magic Kingdom if you prefer it to Electric Umbrella.

2 deli sandwiches with coleslaw	$12.98
2 Children's Meals (come with drinks)	$6.98
Adults drink own beverages or order water	
Total	**$19.96 + tax**

Option #4 Grocery List

Doughnuts	$10.00
1 gallon orange juice	$3.50
1 gallon milk	$3.00
Cereal	$3.00

Fruit	$6.00
Health shakes/Instant breakfast shakes (6-pack)	$6.00
Bagels	$3.50
2 packages of sandwich meat	$5.00
1 package of cheese slices	$2.50
1 jar of jelly	$3.00
1 jar of peanut butter	$3.00
2 loaves of bread	$2.00
1 bag of chips	$2.50
2 four-packs of pudding cups	$3.00
1 microwavable mac & cheese (box of 10)	$8.00
8 pieces of fruit	$9.00
1 box of snack cakes	$1.50
16 drinks (generic sodas and juice boxes)	$3.50

Option #4 Totals

• 5 Breakfasts	$35.00
• 4 Lunches	$43.00
• 4 Dinners	$80.84
Grand total	**$158.84**
$ per meal (÷13)	$12.22
$ per person/meal (÷52)	$3.05

Option #5

All Meals in WDW Counter-Service Restaurants

- 5 Breakfasts: At hotel food court in a Value Resort
- 4 Lunches: At counter-service restaurants in the theme parks
- 4 Dinners: At counter-service restaurants in the theme parks

Breakfast: Days 1, 3, & 5

2 pancake platters with bacon or sausage	$9.98
2 Children's Plates (4 to choose from)	$7.18
Drink own beverages or order water	
Total per day	**$17.16 + tax**

Breakfast: Days 2 & 4

2 platters with eggs, home fries, biscuit, and sausage	$11.18
2 Children's Plates (4 to choose from)	$7.18
Drink own beverages or order water	
Total per day	**$18.36 + tax**

Lunch: Day 1. Cosmic Ray's in Magic Kingdom

2 chicken strips with fries	$12.98
2 Children's Meals (come with drinks)	$6.98
Adults drink own beverages or order water	
Total	**$19.96 + tax**

Lunch: Day 2. Electric Umbrella in Epcot

2 deli sandwiches with coleslaw	$12.98
2 Children's Meals (come with drinks)	$6.98
Adults drink own beverages or order water	
Total:	**$19.96 + tax**

Lunch: Day 3. Toy Story Pizza Planet in Disney–MGM Studios*

2 pepperoni pizzas	$11.58
2 cheese pizzas	$10.98
Drink own beverages or order water	
Total	**$22.56 + tax**

*Consider this lunch a treat for the kids (more expensive per person)

Lunch: Day 4. Tusker House in Disney's Animal Kingdom

1 fried chicken sandwich with fries	$6.99
1 rotisserie chicken with mashed potatoes and vegetable	$7.99

2 Children's Meals (come with drinks)	$6.98
Adults drink own beverages or order water	
Total	*$21.96 + tax*

Dinner: Day 1. Pecos Bill's in Magic Kingdom

2 quarter-pound cheeseburgers with fries	$11.38
2 Children's Meals (come with drinks)	$6.98
Adults drink own beverages or order water	
Total	*$18.36 + tax*

Dinner: Day 2. Cantina de San Angel in Epcot

2 Tacos al Carbon (chicken tacos with refried beans)	$13.98
2 Children's Meals (come with drinks)	$6.98
Adults drink own beverages or order water	
Total	*$20.96 + tax*

Dinner: Day 3. ABC Commissary in Disney-MGM Studios

2 fish and chips	$13.58
2 Children's Meals (come with drinks)	$6.98
Adults drink own beverages or order water	
Total	*$20.56 + tax*

Dinner: Day 4. Electric Umbrella in Epcot

Note: Restaurants in Animal Kingdom generally close before dinnertime (see "Note" after "Dinner: Day 4" in "Option #4," above).

2 deli sandwiches with coleslaw	$12.98
2 Children's Meals (come with drinks)	$6.98
Adults drink own beverages or order water	
Total	*$19.96 + tax*

Option #5 Grocery List

38 soft drinks (optional)	$8.35

Option #5 Totals (including optional soft drinks)

Breakfast	$88.20 + tax
Lunch	$86.64 + tax
Dinner	$81.59 + tax
Grand total	**$260.83 + tax**
$ per meal (÷13)	$20.06 + tax
$ per person/meal (÷52)	$5.02

Option #6
All Meals in Restaurants

*(Be sure to make advance reservations for your sit-down lunches.
See Chapter Three.)*

- 5 Breakfasts: At hotel food court in a Value Resort
- 4 Lunches: At sit-down restaurants in the theme parks (with 15% tip added)
- 4 Dinners: At counter-service restaurants in the theme parks

Breakfast: Days 1, 3, & 5

2 pancake platters with bacon or sausage	$9.98
2 Children's Plates (4 to choose from)	$7.18
Drink own beverages or order water	
Total per day	*$17.16 + tax*

Breakfast: Days 2 & 4

2 platters with eggs, home fries, biscuit, and sausage	$11.18
2 Children's Plates (4 to choose from)	$7.18
Drink own beverages or order water	
Total per day	*$18.36 + tax*

Lunch: Day 1. Tony's Town Square in Magic Kingdom

2 Panini con Pollo	$22.98
2 Children's Plates (come with drinks)	$9.98
Adults drink water	
Total ($32.96 + 15% tip)	*$37.90 + tax*

Lunch: Day 2. Le Cellier in Epcot

2 open-face sirloin steak sandwiches	$23.98
2 children's cheeseburgers and fries	$9.98
All drink water	
Total ($33.96 + 15% tip)	*$39.05 + tax*

Lunch: Day 3. The Hollywood Brown Derby in Disney-MGM Studios

1 10 oz. NY Strip Steak with mashed potatoes	$17.99
1 Barbeque Breast of Chicken Salad	$14.49
2 Children's Plates (come with drinks)	$9.98
Adults drink water	
Total ($42.46 + 15% tip)	*$48.83 + tax*

Lunch: Day 4. Rainforest Café in Disney's Animal Kingdom

1 Planet Earth Pasta	$12.99

1 Mogambo Shrimp	$17.99
2 Children's Plates (come with drinks)	$11.98
Adults drink water	
Total ($42.96 + 15% tip)	*$49.40 + tax*

Dinner: Day 1. Pecos Bill's in Magic Kingdom

2 quarter-pound cheeseburgers with fries	$11.38
2 Children's Meals (come with drinks)	$6.98
Adults drink own beverages or order water	
Total	*$18.36 +tax*

Dinner: Day 2. Cantina de San Angel in Epcot

2 Tacos al Carbon (chicken tacos with refried beans)	$13.98
2 Children's Meals (come with drinks)	$6.98
Adults drink own beverages or order water	
Total	*$20.96 + tax*

Dinner: Day 3. ABC Commissary in Disney-MGM Studios

2 fish and chips	$13.58
2 Children's Meals (come with drinks)	$6.98
Adults drink own beverages or order water	
Total	*$20.56 + tax*

Dinner: Day 4. Electric Umbrella in Epcot

Note: Restaurants in Animal Kingdom generally close before dinnertime (see "Note" after "Dinner: Day 4" in "Option #4," above).

2 deli sandwiches with coleslaw	$12.98
2 Children's Meals (come with drinks)	$6.98
Adults drink own beverages or order water	
Total	*$19.96 + tax*

Option #6 Grocery List

| 28 soft drinks (optional) | $6.15 |

Option #6 Totals (including optional soft drinks)

Breakfast	$88.20 + tax
Lunch	$175.18 (including 15% tips) + tax
Dinner	$79.84 + tax
Grand total	**$349.37 + tax**
$ per meal (÷13)	$26.87
$ per person/meal (÷52)	$6.72

As you can see, eating all your meals in restaurants for four days could easily cost you over $350. And keep in mind that the $350 doesn't include a penny for appetizers, desserts, or drinks that don't come free with the kids' meals. Add these items on and you could easily almost double your meal costs.

If you look at the chart on page 150, you'll see that you can save over $275 during a four-day period just by bringing your own food for breakfast, lunch, and dinner. Spending $350 on meals for four days is equivalent to a month's grocery bill for many families of four. That's too rich for our blood.

Extra Tips for Planning, Budgeting from "Disney on a Dime"

What's important? Most people have to make choices when they go on vacation, because they can't afford everything that might be fun to do or see. You have to decide what is most important to you and your family. Are you going to Disney World for fine dining and a luxurious hotel? Or do you just want to have fun and see Mickey? If you just want to see the parks and have fun, budget low on your hotel stay and food.

> *Note:* Our kids don't enjoy a hamburger any more at Disney World than they do at home. In fact, most little kids will see eating as an obstacle to having fun. Don't waste money on something they won't miss.

Play with your budget. See what it looks like with different features added or taken away. Calculate a "bare bones" budget, a moderate budget, and maybe a wish budget and see how each fits with your plans. Then make adjustments. If you discover that you can save $300 by staying offsite, you may want to splurge a little more on food in the parks — or stay an extra day. You'll never know how much it will cost or how much you can ultimately afford until you sit down and do the math.

Consider a Character Meal. If you want to splurge and give the kids a meal they will enjoy and remember, schedule a Character Meal. They are filling, fun and something you can do hardly anyplace else on earth. (See "Lunch and Dinner" section, *Chapter Three* for details.)

You gotta eat anyway. When preparing your food budget, remember that your family would be spending money on food even if you stayed home. Calculate the difference between your regular food budget and your vacation food budget when figuring the extra money you need for your trip. For example, if your family already budgets $100 a week for groceries and you calculate that your meals at Disney will be $250, simply subtract the $100 from the $250 to know how much extra ($150) you will need to budget for your vacation meals.

Free planning tools. Get some help from various unofficial web sites, as well as Disney itself. At www.wdwplanner.com, you will find a free downloadable program in Excel® spreadsheet format, courtesy of a fan who goes by the moniker "choppertester." It's designed to help you plan your expenses and let's you see immediately the effect on your total expenditures of changing any element in your plan.

For current menus (with prices) of all the WDW eateries, visit www.allears-net.com. The site also contains a treasure trove of useful articles and tips for a Disney World vacation.

Taxes and tips. Disney World is situated in two counties, Osceola and Orange. The tax you pay depends on which one you happen to be in when you make a purchase. You won't go wrong budget-wise if you count on paying the higher rates, 7% for sales tax and 13% for lodging. You will also want to budget an additional 15% to 20% for tips when you eat at a sit-down restaurants. If you don't budget for them, they could really come back to "bite" you.

> *Note:* Some foods that are sold from carts have the tax included in the price.

Be prepared. As with most things in life, anything can and may go wrong on vacation. Have a credit card or a reserve of cash or traveler's checks stashed away to cover contingencies like a flat tire or sprained ankle. Just because you're on vacation doesn't mean that you are immune to life. The difference between things going bad at home and things going bad on vacation is that you aren't at home and could end up stranded. Be prepared.

Plan ahead, pay ahead. Pay most of your vacation expenses before you leave home, and you can really relax while you're away. Here's a brief recap of the tips you'll find discussed in detail in earlier chapters.

> ***Theme park tickets.*** Buy them online, over the phone, or at the Disney Store. The clock doesn't start ticking on them until you use them for the first time. Buy a ticket every couple of months and keep them in a safe place. (See *Chapter Four*.)

> ***Lodging.*** Some online sites actually require upfront payment. In other cases, it's up to you. If you book through Disney's Central Reservations Office, for example, you have to put down a deposit and

can pay off the balance over time (see *Chapters Two* and *Six*).

Transportation. If you're flying and buy tickets online, they usually have to be purchased within 24 hours of your booking. If you're driving, use the weeks and months before your vacation to get your vehicle in shape for the road (see *Chapter Two*).

Food. The water, soft drinks, and nonperishable food items for your meals on the road, snacks in the parks, and any meals you plan to eat in your hotel room can be bought at least six months before your trip to Disney World. Buy extra cases of water and soda, cans of ravioli, or mac and cheese as you save the money for them. And don't forget about that new or extra cooler you may need (see *Chapter Three*).

Souvenirs. Buy them ahead and bring them with you. The kids will never know the difference, and you'll save by getting them at clearance prices. Check online and in stores throughout the year (see *Chapter Five*).

Read and re-read the other chapters in this book to help you plan and save on every facet of your trip.

Track as you go. Review your receipts at the end of the day to get a true look at your expenses versus your budget. This can help to prevent you from spending most of your money early on and not having any left for special things that you wanted to buy or do at the end of the trip.

Keep your receipts. Keep all the receipts from your trip together. Have a special bag or place in your wallet or luggage where every single receipt can go during your trip. Use a small notebook or index card to record any cash payments you made where you didn't get a receipt, such as your tip to the bellhop. This is a great way to see how much you actually spend while you are on vacation. Just be sure you keep every receipt — for gas, souvenirs, snacks, trips to the grocery store, and yes, even that one water you bought in the park. When you return home, you can either celebrate your budget success or learn from your mistakes and apply them to your next vacation.

> *Tip:* If you use a financial program like Quicken®, you can code all your WDW expenses (for example, "Disney 2006") and print out a detailed accounting.

Before you leave for Disney turn down the heat or air conditioning, along with your water heater. Do not turn the heat or a/c off if you think a freeze or a heat wave may occur during your absence, but do turn it down to an extremely low level. If you leave for a week, you could knock 25% off of your utility bills for the time that you are gone. Do the same with the water heater. Otherwise, it will keep right on heating your water even though there is no one at home to use it. Turn down the temperature or turn it off altogether.

- Packing Lists

- Should We Pack the Stroller?

- Extra Tips

WHAT TO PACK

Packing efficiently for your trip can save money in the long run. If you have to run out and buy things that you forgot to pack while on vacation, you may get stuck paying tourist prices for simple toiletries, medicine, or articles of clothing. This comprehensive list will help you to pack thoroughly for your family.

Bear in mind that Orlando weather can be very changeable. While you can count on heat, humidity, and thundershowers in the summer, winter weather (November through March) is much less predictable. It can be mild and pleasant or downright cold, sometimes within the same week.

> *Note:* We include some items (like sunblock and hats) in more than one list to remind you to take the item with you when you go to the theme parks.

Clothing

- [ ] Shirts
- [ ] Shorts
- [ ] Pants
- [ ] Belts
- [ ] Socks
- [ ] Undergarments
- [ ] Pajamas/nightclothes
- [ ] Swimsuits
- [ ] Sweaters or sweatshirts

- [ ] Windbreakers
- [ ] Rain ponchos
- [ ] Hats: A must for everyone in the hot Florida sun.
- [ ] Sandals
- [ ] Walking shoes
- [ ] Flip-flops
- [ ] Water shoes
- [ ] Dress shoes*
- [ ] Panty hose*
- [ ] Evening dresses or suits*

*You'll need these if you plan to go out to an upscale restaurant or club.

Personal Items

- [ ] Contact lenses
- [ ] Prescription glasses
- [ ] Sunglasses: Another must
- [ ] Glasses/lens cases

Toiletries, Cosmetics, Medication

- [ ] Shampoo
- [ ] Conditioner
- [ ] Body wash/bar of soap
- [ ] Kids' shampoo/body wash
- [ ] Hair brushes/combs
- [ ] Ponytail bands and barrettes
- [ ] Hair styling products
- [ ] Deodorant
- [ ] Razor and blades
- [ ] Shaving gel or cream
- [ ] Toothbrushes

- [ ] Toothpaste
- [ ] Toothpaste for kids
- [ ] Dental floss
- [ ] Mouthwash
- [ ] Body lotion
- [ ] Sunblock for adults and kids: Another must
- [ ] Aloe Vera gel for possible sunburn treatment
- [ ] Make-up remover
- [ ] Facial moisturizer
- [ ] Lip balm
- [ ] Cotton swabs
- [ ] Cotton balls
- [ ] Nail clippers
- [ ] Nail file
- [ ] Nail polish
- [ ] Nail polish remover
- [ ] Tweezers
- [ ] Perfume/Cologne
- [ ] Make-up
- [ ] Contact lens solution
- [ ] Eye drops
- [ ] Feminine hygiene products
- [ ] Basic first-aid kit
- [ ] Bandage strips
- [ ] Cough drops
- [ ] Laxative
- [ ] Antacids
- [ ] Stomach soothing remedies
- [ ] Anti-itch cream
- [ ] Muscle pain relieving cream or heat pack
- [ ] Motion sickness remedy

- [ ] Blister treatment items
- [ ] Prescription medications
- [ ] Adult pain medication
- [ ] Vitamins for adults and kids
- [ ] Cold medication
- [ ] Cough medication
- [ ] Children's/infants' pain killer, fever reducer
- [ ] Allergy medication

Items for Babies and Toddlers

- [ ] Diapers
- [ ] Moist towelettes
- [ ] Spill-proof cups
- [ ] Bottles
- [ ] Formula or breast pump
- [ ] Pacifiers
- [ ] Diaper rash cream
- [ ] Teething medicine
- [ ] Pain reliever/fever reducer
- [ ] Baby nail clippers
- [ ] Baby lotion
- [ ] Baby shampoo/body wash
- [ ] Baby powder
- [ ] Disposable bibs
- [ ] Baby food and snacks
- [ ] Disposable baby spoons, bowls, and cups
- [ ] Swim diapers
- [ ] Sling or other strap-on baby carrier
- [ ] Car seat
- [ ] Stroller (if not renting one in the parks)

For the Theme Parks

- [ ] PARK TICKETS/Annual Passes!!!
- [ ] Ponchos or umbrellas
- [ ] Hats
- [ ] Sunglasses
- [ ] Autograph books
- [ ] Pens
- [ ] Pins for trading
- [ ] Park guidebooks
- [ ] Pennies and quarters for penny and quarter presses
- [ ] Water bottles (canteens or Camelbak®s)
- [ ] Water purifier
- [ ] Hand sanitizer
- [ ] Camera
- [ ] Video camera
- [ ] Camera bags
- [ ] Extra videotapes
- [ ] Extra film or memory cards
- [ ] Extra batteries
- [ ] Handheld fan/mister
- [ ] Walkie-talkies
- [ ] Tissue
- [ ] Sunblock stick
- [ ] Headache medicine
- [ ] Baby items
- [ ] Beach towels (for water parks)
- [ ] Floats and noodles (for water parks)
- [ ] Goggles (for water parks)
- [ ] Glow bracelets and necklaces
- [ ] Glow toys
- [ ] Bug repellent

☐ Snacks
☐ Water
☐ Small collapsible cooler
☐ Bag/backpack to carry your park items

Kitchen and On-the-Road Meal Items

☐ Self-seal plastic bags: large and sandwich sized
☐ Paper plates
☐ Paper towels/napkins
☐ Paper cups
☐ Plastic cutlery
☐ Plastic disposable bowls
☐ Straws (Reminder: these are not allowed in Disney's Animal Kingdom)
☐ Microwave-safe bowls
☐ Serving spoon and fork
☐ Blue gel ice packs
☐ Dish soap
☐ Sponges
☐ Large- to medium-sized cooler for car or mini-portable fridge
☐ Powdered instant flavored drink mix
☐ Soft drinks
☐ Water
☐ Juice
☐ Bread or sandwich rolls
☐ Lunchmeat and cheese
☐ Packets of condiments
☐ Lettuce and tomato cut up in plastic bags
☐ Snack crackers
☐ Chips
☐ Granola bars
☐ Trail mix

- [ ] Fruit
- [ ] Fruit gummies or roll-ups
- [ ] Beef jerky
- [ ] Peanut butter
- [ ] Jelly or jam
- [ ] Microwave popcorn
- [ ] Instant oatmeal
- [ ] Cold cereal
- [ ] Instant soup mix
- [ ] Hot cocoa mix
- [ ] Salt and pepper

*Buy cold items, like yogurt, milk, and frozen foods that you don't need on the road, when you get to Orlando.

Car Ride Items

- [ ] Road maps and driving directions
- [ ] Car registration
- [ ] Proof of insurance
- [ ] CDs
- [ ] DVD or video player
- [ ] DVDs or videos
- [ ] AC adapter (if needed)
- [ ] Headphones
- [ ] New books, toys, and games for kids and babies on the road
- [ ] Handheld video games
- [ ] Tissues
- [ ] Hand sanitizer
- [ ] Barf bags
- [ ] Flashlights
- [ ] Phone chargers
- [ ] Camera-battery chargers

- [ ] Small trash bags
- [ ] Pillows
- [ ] Small blanket for each person
- [ ] Magazines or sewing project for mom
- [ ] Cooler with ice and cold drinks
- [ ] Sandwich items
- [ ] Snacks for the road
- [ ] Paper towels or napkins
- [ ] Moist towelettes
- [ ] Guidebooks for the parks

Miscellaneous Items

- [ ] Health insurance info
- [ ] Prescription insurance info
- [ ] Doctors' phone numbers
- [ ] Copy of prescription for eyeglasses or contact lenses
- [ ] Address book
- [ ] Postage stamps
- [ ] Email addresses of friends and family
- [ ] Coupons
- [ ] Discount cards
- [ ] Sewing kit
- [ ] Laundry detergent (tablets)/fabric softener (sheets)
- [ ] Stain stick or stain treatment wipes
- [ ] Laundry bags or pop-up hamper
- [ ] Pens
- [ ] Notepads
- [ ] Compact or inexpensive fishing gear (to fish on WDW property)

Last Minute Items

- [ ] Confirmation numbers for lodging and restaurant reservations

- [ ] Cell phones & battery chargers
- [ ] Car and house keys
- [ ] Extra set of car and house keys
- [ ] Driver's licenses
- [ ] Social security cards
- [ ] Glasses
- [ ] Sunglasses
- [ ] Credit cards
- [ ] Traveler's checks
- [ ] Cash
- [ ] Checkbook
- [ ] Wallet
- [ ] Purse
- [ ] Jewelry
- [ ] Watches
- [ ] Plane tickets
- [ ] Travel itinerary
- [ ] Annual Passholder and AAA discount list (if applicable)

Extra Tips for Planning, Packing from "Disney on a Dime"

Buy shoes and equipment well ahead of your trip to make sure everything fits and works as it should.

Footwear. Do not rush out the day before your trip and try to find shoes for Disney World. People make this mistake all too often. If you live in the north and need sandals in the middle of the winter, you'll have a tough time finding any. Even if you just need a new pair of sneakers, you're better off buying them several weeks in advance and breaking them in. You can easily walk five miles your first day at Disney World. In new shoes, this can translate into mega-blisters.

Camera or video camera. Learn how to operate your new equipment and try it out before you hit the road. Check that you have all the equipment you need and know what kind of batteries it takes and what kind of film or recording device it needs. Tape some pre-vacation shots and have them processed to be sure everything is working. Finding out on your first day at Disney World that you don't have the proper charger, tape, or film for your new device would be an unmagical start to your vacation.

Two-way radios are very popular in the parks because they help friends and family members keep track of each other when they split up to do various things. Test these devices out to ascertain their true range and see how long the batteries last. Buy devices that have several channels and try a range of settings. Most people in the parks will be using the default setting and that leads to interference. Program your radios to a unique setting beforehand.

> *$$aver Tip:* Shopping well in advance also gives you time to look for the best price and take advantage of sales.

Earplugs for kids. Pack earplugs if you have a child who is easily startled by loud noises. You'll find them at most discount stores and pharmacies. The plugs are made of a soft foam material you can roll up and place in the child's ear.

> *Tip:* If your child won't wear earplugs, consider packing a portable music player, headphones, and your child's favorite CD. The music will camouflage any startling sounds.

Label all valuables. Label your camera, video camera, wallet, stroller, or on anything that you could possibly misplace that is of value with your name, hotel, home address, and cell phone number. If you lose or misplace them, the labels will make it easy to get them back to you. Nine times out of ten, when you lose something at Disney World, you get it back. It must have something to do with the Disney magic. Or maybe it just attracts honest people.

Bring along some hand-held games. Waiting in line is inevitable at Disney World. Even with FASTPASSes and low attendance, you and your family will be stuck in a line at some point. How do you keep the kids from kicking the person in front of you or climbing on the rails? A hand-held electronic game can be a great to keep them focused on something other than standing still in between railings. It helps them pass the time a little faster and keeps their spirits up.

Or try some other distractions. If electronic games aren't your thing, one or more of the following may do the trick:

Play games such as "I spy" or "paper-rock-scissors" with your kids.

Talk about your favorite rides so far and what fun things you've done.

Look for hidden Mickeys. A handy guidebook called "Hidden Mickeys" is available in the stores in the parks (and ahead of time in bookstores and online). It can help you and your kids spot nearly 500 hidden Mickeys all around Walt Disney World.

Review your itinerary and map and talk about the things you are going to do later. If you have downloaded park maps onto your Palm Pilot or cell phone, let the kids explore the virtual maps.

$$aver Tip: Go to www.pocketdisney.com for free cell phone and PDA downloads.

Check out the projected weather before you leave. It is impossible to foresee the weather in Florida on any extremely accurate level, but you should be able to get an idea of what to expect during your stay by checking one or more of the weather sites on the Internet, such as www.weather.com. The site's historical data will show you the averages, highs, and lows over a 30-year history of the area. This is a great way to see when the weather is mildest, hottest, coldest, rainiest, driest, and so on. Check in out well in advance to help you with your packing. Then check the 10-day forecast the day before you leave to get a more specific idea of what to expect on your vacation.

Note: If the historical data shows that the weather can dip down to 50 degrees, pack at least one set of warm clothing for each member of the family. Then, if the temperature drops suddenly while you're there, you will not have to buy new clothes, as most unprepared visitors are forced to do.

Should We Pack the Stroller?

A stroller is a must at Disney World if you have little ones. Even if your kids are five to eight, a stroller is good to have. As mentioned before, your family will walk several miles each day at WDW, and the little ones will have to take a lot more steps than you because their legs are so much shorter. Little kids cannot take that much walking for a long period of time.

Stroller Options

If you are driving, bring the stroller. If you are flying, you have a number of options:

Bring your stroller

Most airlines will allow you to check your stroller in as luggage or check it at the entrance to the plane. Checking the stroller at the entrance is a good option if you have a layover or will need some help carting your luggage around.

> *Note:* Big strollers are nice to have and can carry two children at once, but be forewarned that it will be slightly difficult to fold them quickly when you are getting on WDW transportation. You don't have to collapse the stroller for the Monorail or the Ferry from the Ticket and Transportation Center to the Magic Kingdom, but you will have to collapse it for the trains, parking lot trams, and buses, as well as on some of the small resort ferries. It isn't a huge hassle, but if you don't need a bulky stroller we would suggest you go with something smaller.

Rent a stroller

You can rent strollers on a daily basis ($8 for a single or $15 for a double) at each of the theme parks. You rent them near each park entrance gate and then simply leave them at the gate when you leave the park. Keep the receipt. If you decide to go to another park on the same day, just show the receipt and pick up another stroller at no additional charge. The receipt is good till the end of the day.

Better yet, get a multi-day discount if you plan to rent a stroller for more than a day. Determine how many days you'll need it and then make the arrangements for your entire visit on day one. Disney World offers a 10% discount for all but the first day, but only if you pay in full on day one. You cannot show a receipt from a previous day and get a discount.

Downsides to rentals:

• You must leave the stroller at each park. That means you have to carry the baby or toddler on transportation between parks and practically everywhere outside of the parks, including your hotel. This can get very tiring very fast.

• The strollers can be uncomfortable for the kids. They are made of hard plastic that can wear on the kids real fast. The only strollers not made of the hard plastic are the ones at Disney-MGM Studios.

• If you are staying for a week or two, you'll waste a fair amount of money.

• You can't rent a stroller to visit Downtown Disney, the Boardwalk, or the resorts. That limits your opportunity to enjoy all that Disney World has to offer.

Buy a disposable stroller

If all you need is a single stroller for one child, consider buying a cheap $12 umbrella stroller. You can get them at any discount or grocery store. They are light, easily collapsible, and very easy to maneuver in a crowded theme park. At the end of the trip, throw the stroller away. You'll have spent less than it would cost you to rent a stroller for two days.

Tip: If your stroller breaks, you can get a hefty umbrella stroller at Once Upon a Toy in Downtown Disney for around $40. That's a lot, but considering the alternatives, it might still be your best bet.

Bring a Backpack Carrier, Too

We have found it helpful to bring both a stroller and a backpack carrier so that we can alternate between parks or from one day to the next. Being confined to a stroller for days at a time can be frustrating for a toddler.

Caution: Some backpack carriers convert into strollers. The extra weight of these devices can be too much to handle. Try out the different kinds and see what fits your situation best.

Special Stroller Tips

• Buy a waterproof stroller cover. You can find stroller covers at Babies R Us and other specialty retailers. In Orlando, it can rain any time, and in the summer you can almost count on a daily shower.

• Cover your stroller whenever you go into a ride or attraction. That blue sky can develop thunderclouds and pour rain while you are enjoying a 30-minute show.

• Don't leave valuables, like your camera, in your stroller. However, you can safely leave diaper bags, backpacks, and coats.

• Take advantage of the stroller to lighten your load. Let it carry backpacks and other paraphernalia, along with your little one.

101 ABSOLUTELY FREE (OR VERY CHEAP) THINGS TO DO AT WDW

Through the years we have compiled a list of some fun things to do at Disney World that cost absolutely nothing or close to it. Many people who spend a lot of money to get to Disney World simply go to the parks, ride the rides, see the shows, and then head on home. Our suggestion is to take the time to take advantage of at least a couple of the special activities and other "extras" that the parks offer ticket holders at no additional cost and also to schedule a couple of days to enjoy some of the free and low-cost things Walt Disney World offers instead of spending all your time in the theme parks.

Some may not seem like big deals to adults but, for kids, they can be among their favorite memories.

Take a Ride

WDW transportation is free and can be fun. It isn't every day that you can ride a monorail, catch a boat, and then jump on a bus in a matter of minutes. Access to transportation is free as long as you have some form of a ticket that you will use or have used at some point. Disney normally is concerned about tickets only in the morning before 10:30 or 11 a.m., when there is heavy traffic going to the parks.

Monorail

• Ride the Monorail to Magic Kingdom and Epcot. Hop in as often as you like. All you need to ride is proof of a multi-day ticket, Annual Pass, or resort key.

• Ride the inner-Monorail track to some of the Deluxe Resorts. View them from the monorail car or get out and walk around.

- Ride up front with the Monorail driver. After this special ride you will receive a free "Monorail co-pilot" certificate.

    Tip: The best time to get a chance to do this is during the middle of the day.

Boats

- Ride the Friendship Boats around Epcot's Crescent Lake and see Epcot's International Gateway, the Boardwalk, WDW's Swan and Dolphin Hotels, and Disney-MGM Studios. Park admission is not required.
- Ride the ferry to and from the Ticket and Transit Center (TTC) and the Magic Kingdom. You can alternate rides between the ferry and the Monorail.
- Ride the ferry from Downtown Disney to Port Orleans and back.
- Ride the resort ferries that tour the Seven Seas Lagoon and the many resorts in the area. Catch them at marinas on the Lagoon.

Bus

- Grab a bus and roam around the entire Walt Disney World Resort. If you don't have a car this is the best way to see the different resorts.

Take a Walk

- Walk from Epcot to Disney-MGM Studios (you don't have to go into either). This is a nice 10- to 15-minute stroll along the Boardwalk.
- Walk from the Contemporary Resort to the Magic Kingdom. This is a very short walk with some great views.

See the Fireworks

Park admission is fairly expensive, but hanging out *near* the parks is absolutely free and open to all.

- Watch the Magic Kingdom fireworks from the TTC area. Near the loading platform of the ferry, you'll enjoy a great view of Cinderella Castle and the fireworks that light up the sky above and around it. The narration and music are piped into the TTC, so you can follow the whole program.
- Watch the Magic Kingdom fireworks from the entrance to the Magic King-

dom or from the Monorail landing directly outside. You do not need to pay to ride the monorail or to stand outside the park entrance. There is a good view here and it is free.

• Watch the Epcot fireworks from the Monorail platform. Stand at the top of the platform and watch the skies. You'll miss the spinning globe and other elements of the show that take place on the lake inside the park, but the fireworks are fun to watch on their own.

• Watch the Epcot fireworks free from the patio of the Boardwalk Inn (second floor).

• Enter Epcot free after the fireworks through the International Gateway. You won't be able to ride any rides, but the park is open for another hour and so are the shops. Walk around in a very relaxing atmosphere and soak in the feel of the different countries in World Showcase.

Visit Downtown Disney

Downtown Disney is virtually a separate park in and of itself. There are so many things to do here that you could easily spend a whole day shopping, playing, and just enjoying the atmosphere. While you are here you can:

• Visit the many Disney specialty shops: The Art of Disney, Disney at Home, Disney's Days of Christmas, Pooh Corner, Disney's Pin Traders (said to be the world's largest trading center), and Team Mickey's Athletic Club.

• Check out the merchandise and displays in World of Disney, the biggest Disney Store in the world. Annual Passholders get 10% off.

• Play in the water fountains (there are two). Let the kids wear their swimsuits and run around in the water jets as they shoot out of the ground.

• Be amazed by free magic tricks at Magic Masters Shop.

   Note: Some activities are seasonal. You can go ice-skating in winter. Skating is free but you'll need to bring your own skates or rent some for a small fee.

• Enjoy the midnight fireworks at Pleasure Island. It doesn't cost a cent to walk through Pleasure Island.

• Listen to the bands that perform nightly at West End Stage Entertainment

• Hunt for "Hidden Mickeys," images of Mickey Mouse camouflaged in Downtown Disney's walls and stores. You can download a free Hidden

Mickeys Mini Hunt, complete with clues and points to be scored from my publisher at www.TheOtherOrlando.com/hunt.html

Pay a long visit to the Lego Imagination Center

Outdoors it offers:

• A 3,000 square foot playground where little ones can run around and whiz down a slide.

• Individual Lego tables where you and the kids can build whatever your imaginations dream up.

• Huge Lego statues. Large dragons, a spaceship, and other creations offer great photo ops and show what you could create if you had a truckload of Legos.

Inside you'll find:

• Both Duplo and Lego tables with plenty of pieces. Playing inside the Center, out of the sun and hubbub, is an especially attractive option when it is hot outside and when you have a very little one.

Let the kids get creative at Once Upon a Toy

• Put Mr. Potato Head together. The Once Upon a Toy shop has a great display of Mr. Potato Head Disney pieces and you can help yourself to them to create your own version of what he should look like. You don't have to buy a thing. Just play.

• Create your own virtual version of the guy or gal on one of the touchscreen monitors that you will find adjacent to the Mr. Potato Head display. When you're done, print out the picture and keep it as a souvenir.

• Go scavenger hunting to answer a quiz that's printed on the back of the printout you got. Search the store for clues, then answer the questions and take the finished sheet to the clerk. You'll get a prize. (It makes a great souvenir!)

• Use the My Little Pony touchscreen monitors to create another picture that you can print out and keep as a souvenir.

• Play with three-dimensional My Little Ponies. Dress them up, add accessories, and give them a spin in their very own "Tea Cup" ride.

Enjoy the BoardWalk

The BoardWalk is an area just outside of Epcot that looks like — what else? — an old boardwalk. It is loaded with shops, clubs, and activities for all ages. There is no admission fee and everything that you can experience here is practically free, except of course, for merchandise, food, and the rentable surreys.

Here you can:

• Park free for three hours. Ask for a pass from the parking attendant.

• Take in your favorite sporting events at the ESPN Club, where they have too many TVs to count. Every booth has a personal LCD TV for your viewing pleasure. You can watch as long as you want absolutely free, but you'll probably want to get a soft drink, especially if other people are waiting for a booth.

• Enjoy the sidewalk performers. At night, the fun begins with jugglers and other street acts vying for the attention of passersby.

• Dance to DJ music at Atlantic Dance Hall. It's open Tuesday through Saturday (closed Sundays and Mondays). There is no admission and no cover charge, but you must be 21 or older to get in.

• Visit Wyland Galleries of Florida to see original works of art. Wyland's marine-life paintings include life-like scenes from the deep. You'll also see Disney collaborative pieces that include Mickey and the gang.

Enjoy Public Activities at the Resorts

Lots of fun activities take place in and around the various WDW resorts that are open to everyone. You don't have to stay in the resort hosting the activity to participate. You don't even have to be a resort guest.

Fort Wilderness Resort

Fort Wilderness probably offers more free and low-cost activities than any other Disney Resort. Take advantage of them.

> *Note:* The parking is free. Just ask for a parking pass at the Guest Relations desk.

• Pet the animals at the Fort Wilderness petting farm.

• Enjoy Fort Wilderness Campground's nightly campfire, where you can join in sing-a-longs, meet Chip and Dale, roast marshmallows, and watch a free classic Disney movie. Bring your own marshmallows and treats or buy them at the Campground.

• Take a hike. Fort Wilderness has some great hiking trails.

• Tour the Blacksmith Shop.

• Check out the draft horses that pull the trolley in the Magic Kingdom. The horses live at Tri-Circle-D Ranch in Fort Wilderness, where you can see them when they're not on duty.

• Ride a pony. At $3, this is close to free.

Other Resorts

• Watch the Electrical Water Pageant. This nightly water parade can be viewed from the TTC and from the beaches of the Polynesian, Grand Floridian, and Contemporary Resorts, as well as from the Ticket and Transportation Center near the Magic Kingdom. You do not need to be a Disney resort guest to walk onto the beach and see the show.

• Walk around the different resorts to explore the beautiful landscaping. The grounds are open to the public.

• Explore the huge lobbies of the Deluxe resorts. Admire the décor, artifacts, and other interesting items that are on display. Ask for a free tour, maps, and highlights.

   Tip: If you have a copy of "Hidden Mickeys," by Steven Barrett, you can take the kids on your own Hidden Mickeys hunts at the resorts.

• Let the kids play awhile at the various resort hotels' themed playgrounds. Each is unique.

• Hunt for penny presses. Every resort has its own penny press. Go from resort to resort and collect the different pennies for souvenirs. You supply the pennies.

• Explore the resort arcades. Every resort has at least one.

• Go fishing (catch and release) at Port Orleans–Riverside. No license is needed on Disney property. You can bring your own poles and supplies. Or rent a cane pole and buy bait there.

   Note: You can also fish at Fort Wilderness and Downtown Disney.

• Watch the torch lighting ceremony at dusk at the Polynesian Great Ceremonial Hall. The ceremony takes place several nights a week. Ask for specific times and days at the front desk, or call 407-824-2000.

- Walk through the torch-lit gardens at the Polynesian Resort.

- Listen to live piano music in the lobby of the Grand Floridian.

- Walk along the beach outside the Polynesian Resort.

- Check out the ladybug release at the Grand Floridian's 1900 Park Fare Herb Garden every Thursday at 11:00 a.m.

- See the Butterfly Garden at Port Orleans–Riverside.

- Take the free Garden Tour at the Yacht and Beach Club Resorts. Call 407-934-8000 for details.

- Visit Parrot Cay Island at the Caribbean Beach Resort. You'll find a playground there and live parrots to admire.

- Watch the giraffes and other animals on the African savannah at Animal Kingdom Lodge. For a special view, go at night and walk out the back of the lobby to Arusha Rock. Ask one of the naturalists there to let you look for animals through a pair of night vision glasses.

- See "Old Faithful" Geyser at the Wilderness Lodge.

- Take advantage of the great photo opportunities at the Value Resorts. Huge statues of Buzz Lightyear or some of the 101 Dalmatians make for great vacation shots.

Enjoy Even More Resort Activities as a Resort Guest

I know it's not fair, but some activities are reserved exclusively for Disney's Resort guests. But it would also be unfair for them to pay the big bucks they shell out and not be able to make exclusive use of at least some of the services they pay for. If you stay onsite, here are a few of the free things that you may be able to do.

- Shape up at the Old Key West Fitness Center. It is free to all Walt Disney World Resort guests.

- Take a tour to search for Hidden Mickeys. Some of the Moderate and Deluxe Resorts offer guided tours to find Hidden Mickeys in the Resort's walls, carpets, lighting, and so on.

    Tip: Non-guests can hunt for them on their own in lobbies, hallways, and other public spaces.

- Get a tour of the resort. At the Grand Floridian, Wilderness Lodge, Animal

Kingdom Lodge, and some of the other Deluxe Resorts, you can arrange for a tour through Guest Services or the Lobby Concierge.

• Take advantage of special activities for the kids, such as craft projects. The reception desk and Guest Services can tell you what's available.

• Enjoy storytelling if it's offered at your resort. The Front Desk can fill you in on availability, place, and times.

• Visit Ol' Man Island if you are staying at Port Orleans. Its three acres offer a pool, whirlpool, playground, and fishin' hole (fishing allowed daily).

• Play basketball free at Fort Wilderness, the Contemporary, and Old Key West.

• Play croquet free at the Beach Club and Boardwalk resorts.

• Play volleyball and tennis free at resorts that have courts.

More Cheap Things to Do Outside the Parks

Note: Walt Disney World is dotted with lakes. A number of the resorts, along with the BoardWalk and Downtown Disney have marinas, where you can rent the watercraft mentioned below. Not all marinas offer every type of craft, so phone to check what is available before you make a trip:

Disney's Beach Club Resort Marina	407-934-8000
Disney's Caribbean Beach Resort Marina	407-934-3400
Disney's Contemporary Resort Marina	407-824-1000
Disney's Port Orleans Resort Marina	407-934-6000
Disney's Grand Floridian Resort & Spa Marina	407-824-3000
Disney's Polynesian Resort Marina	407-824-2000
Disney's Wilderness Lodge Marina	407-824-3200
Disney's Yacht Club Resort	407-934-7000
Disney's Fort Wilderness Resort & Campground Marina	407-824-2900
Disney's Old Key West Resort Marina	407-827-7700
Disney's Coronado Springs Resort Marina	407-939-1000
Downtown Disney® Marketplace Marina	407-939-2648

• Rent paddle boats ($7 for half an hour).

• Rent canoes at Fort Wilderness ($7 for half an hour).

- Rent pedal boats at a number of resort marinas (seat 4, $7 for half an hour).

- Rent hydro bikes at the Swan and Dolphin hotels ($8 for half an hour).

- Rent kayaks at Coronado Springs, Port Orleans–Riverside, and Fort Wilderness ($7 for half an hour).

- Take a wagon ride at Fort Wilderness Campground ($8 for adults, $4 for children).

- Rent bikes at Fort Wilderness, the BoardWalk, and many of the Moderate and Deluxe Resorts (under $10 for half an hour).

- Ride the kiddie train at Downtown Disney ($2).

- Ride the small carousel at Downtown Disney ($2).

- Play carnival games on Wildwood Landing at the BoardWalk ($1 to $3).

- Watch a movie at the AMC Theatre located in Downtown Disney. Adult Annual Passholders get $2 off after 6:00 p.m.

- Take a free look at the Walt Disney World Speedway, adjacent to the Magic Kingdom parking lot. Call 800-BE-PETTY for information.

- Play miniature golf at Disney World's Fantasia Gardens or Winter Summerland courses (18 holes, adults about $11, children about $9).

Free Things to Do in the Theme Parks that You May Have Overlooked

The purpose of this section is to point out free things to do in the theme parks that most people overlook. Yes, you pay to get in to the parks, so these "extras" are technically included in the price of admission. But relatively few people take advantage of them. Have more fun and get more for your money by doing at least a few of them. They're all things you would never expect to get for free. In fact, you'd probably be willing to pay for them (if you had the money) because they can add a lot of magic to your visit.

> *$$aver Tip*: Some of these activities offer prizes that can substitute for an expensive store-bought souvenir.

Magic Kingdom

- Enjoy free samples at the Main Street Confectionery. You can watch them make the candy while you munch.

- Visit the horses at the Car Barn on Main Street.

• Get free embroidery on your purchases — or a Disney hat that you bring with you — at the Chapeau on Main Street U.S.A.

Epcot

• See and try the latest in technology for free at Innoventions.

• Get free pictures and email by playing with the various machines in Kodak Image Works' "What If" labs.

• Enjoy "Dream Chasers," a free virtual reality ride near the exit of *Test Track*. Most people just walk on by this "extra" ride.

• Try your skills at the Mission Launch simulation at the end of the *Mission: SPACE* ride.

• Enjoy free soft drinks from around the world at Ice Station Cool.

And just for kids:

• Do the Kidcot Fun Stop projects. The kids can visit every country in World Showcase, do a craft project at each one (for example, make a mask in Mexico, and get a stamp. Once they collect stamps from every country, they get a prize. They can also do Kidcot projects in Future World.

• Go on a scavenger hunt. The "Kid's Guide to Epcot Scavenger Hunt" is available at the park entrances. Answer several questions about the rides and countries in order to solve a final riddle and, possibly, get a prize from Guest Relations.

• Don a chef's hat and make some cookies as part of Nestle's Junior Chef Program in The Land pavilion. Kids must be between three and ten years old. All participants receive a free hat and cookies.

• Play in the interactive water fountains. Be sure to bring swimsuits and towels for your little ones.

Disney–MGM Studios

• Be an extra in the *Indiana Jones Epic Stunt Spectacular* show. When they ask for volunteers, jump around and wave your hands vigorously to increase your chances of being selected. This is a free experience that only a few can enjoy.

• Try for the "hot seat" at *Who Wants to be a Millionaire–Play It!*

Disney's Animal Kingdom

• Watch veterinarians tend to the medical needs of animals at *Rafiki's Planet*

Watch. You might even get to see an operation.

• Participate in Family Fun projects at stations located throughout the park. These are similar to the Scavenger Hunt at Epcot. Find and do everything as you are directed and you'll get a prize.

Special Seasonal Theme Park Events

Throughout the year, Disney holds special events in its parks to help it draw bigger crowds. During these events, guests can experience many free things that are available at no other time. By planning your visit to coincide with an event, you'll be able to enjoy more free activities, experience more magic, and ultimately get more for the price of your admission.

In Epcot

International Flower and Garden Festival (Mid-April through May)

• Admire special flower displays and topiaries throughout the park.

• Enjoy free presentations by garden experts.

• Watch the daily butterfly and ladybug releases. Your kids can participate in letting them go at either or both of these events.

• Other free activities for the kids during this event include a Digging Maze and a Space Garden.

Food and Wine Festival (October through mid-November)

• Rock to big names like the Beach Boys, the Temptations, and Chubby Checker at free concerts in the Eat to the Beat concert series in World Showcase. The free concerts are held several times a day.

• Enjoy free culinary classes and demonstrations.

• Take the kids to free beekeeping and peanut farming demonstrations, then let them take a look at the pumpkins shaped like Mickey Mouse.

Christmas around the World (Late November through December)

• Candlelight Processional. Celebrities (a different one each day) read the Christmas Story, accompanied by a choir and a 50-piece orchestra. (It's free but you have to make reservations ahead of time to get a seat.)

• Holiday storytellers. Individuals from each country in World Showcase tell a Christmas story that reflects their culture.

In Disney-MGM Studios

MGM Star Wars Weekends (weekends from mid-May through mid-June)

• Meet the "stars" from *Star Wars*. You can count on seeing at least ten people — stars, designers, etc. — connected with this popular series.

• Let the kids earn a certificate in swordsmanship at the Jedi Training Academy.

MGM Soap Opera Weekend (a weekend in November)

• Meet the celebrities from your favorite soaps.

Osborne Family Spectacle of Lights (Late November through December)

• Get into the Christmas spirit by walking through this award-winning outdoor display. Millions of holiday lights decorate selected streets, transforming them into a vast holiday display.

And One Offbeat Freebie

• Sit through a Disney Vacation Club (DVC) presentation and get a tour of the properties to see how the other half lives. DVC is Disney's timeshare operation, and some of the nicest resorts at WDW are DVC properties (check www.Disneyworld.com for a list of them). You can sign up for a presentation in any of the parks (look for the DVC sign) or at any DVC property.

$$aver Tip: Most presentations offer a free breakfast.

APPENDIX:
PHONE NUMBERS & MAPS

General Information	407-824-4321
Reservations	
Central Reservations	800-828-0228
	407-934-7639
Disney Resort Reservations	407-939-6244
Annual Passholder Info & Reservations	407-560-7277
Dining Reservations	407-939-3463
Guest Relations	407-824-4321
Other Useful Numbers	
Babysitting (within 30 days only)	407-828-0920
Disney Cruise Line®	800-939-2784
Disney Dining Experience	407-566-5858
Disney Fishing Info & Reservations	407-939-7529
Disney Golf	407-939-4653
Disney Kennels	407-824-6568
Disney's Wide World of Sports® Box Office	407-939-4263
Hearing Impaired Information	407-939-7670

Downtown Disney

Cirque du Soleil	407-934-7639
DisneyQuest® Indoor Interactive Theme Park	407-828-4600
Downtown Disney® Area	407-939-2648
Pleasure Island	407-939-2648

Resort Front Desk Numbers (not for reservations)

Value Resorts

Disney's All-Star Movies Resort	407-939-7000
Disney's All-Star Music Resort	407-939-6000
Disney's All-Star Sports Resort	407-939-5000
Disney's Pop Century Resort	407-938-4000

Moderate Resorts

Disney's Caribbean Beach Resort	407-934-3400
Disney's Coronado Springs Resort	407-939-1000
Disney's Port Orleans Resort–French Quarter	407-934-5000
Disney's Port Orleans Resort–Riverside	407-934-6000

Deluxe Resorts

Disney's Animal Kingdom Lodge	407-938-3000
Disney's Contemporary Resort	407-824-1000
Disney's Grand Floridian Resort and Spa	407-824-3000
Disney's Polynesian Resort	407-824-2000
Disney's Wilderness Lodge	407-824-3200

Disney Vacation Club   800-800-9100

Disney Vacation Club Resorts

Disney's Saratoga Springs Resort & Spa	407-827-1100
Disney's Beach Club Resort	407-934-8000
Disney's BoardWalk Inn	407-939-5100
Disney's BoardWalk Villas	407-939-5100

Disney's Old Key West Resort	407-827-7700
Disney's Yacht Club Resort	407-934-7000
The Villas at Disney's Wilderness Lodge	407-824-3200

Shades of Green   407-824-3600
   (for US active and retired military personnel
   and their families)

Walt Disney World Dolphin Hotel
   Reservations   888-625-5144
   Front Desk   407-934-4000

Walt Disney World Swan Hotel
   Reservations   888-625-5144
   Front Desk   407-934-3000

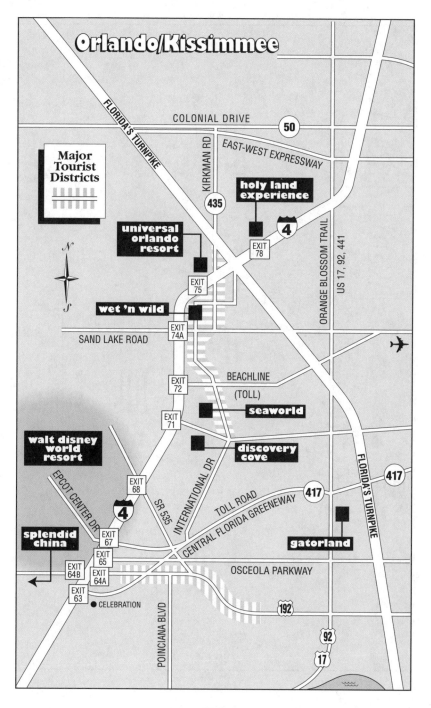

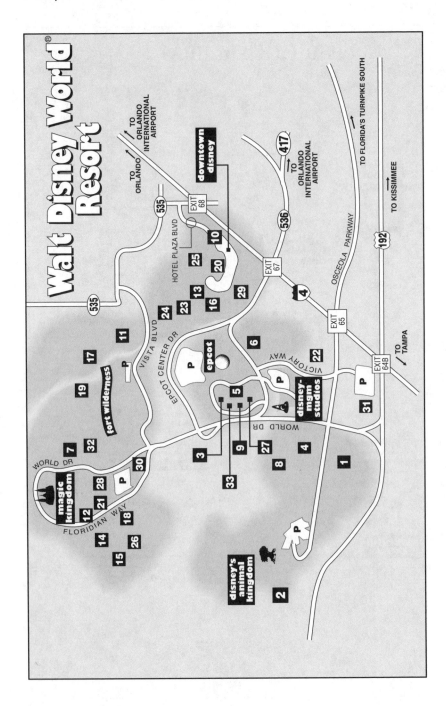

1 All-Star Resorts
2 Animal Kingdom Lodge
3 Beach Club
4 Blizzard Beach
5 BoardWalk
6 Caribbean Beach
7 Contemporary
8 Coronado Springs
9 Dolphin
10 Downtown Disney
11 Eagle Pines Golf Course
12 Grand Floridian
13 Lake Buena Vista Golf Course
14 Magnolia Golf Course
15 Oak Trails Golf Course
16 Old Key West
17 Osprey Ridge Golf Course
18 Palm Golf Course

19 Pioneer Hall
20 Pleasure Island, in Downtown Disney
21 Polynesian
22 Pop Century
23 Port Orleans French Quarter
24 Port Orleans Riverside
25 Saratoga Springs
26 Shades of Green
27 Swan
28 Transportation and Ticket Center
29 Typhoon Lagoon
30 WDW Speedway
31 Wide World of Sports
32 Wilderness Lodge
33 Yacht Club
P Parking

INDEX

Our Guarantee

We are so confident that the strategies we lay out in *Disney on a Dime* can save you and your family *at least* $200 on a week's vacation to Disney World, that we guarantee it.

If you find that our strategies don't work for you, simply tear off the front cover of the book and write a short note on the back of it telling us when you visited Walt Disney World, what you tried, and why it didn't work. Then send us the cover with your receipt for the book (so we'll know how much you paid) to:

> Disney on a Dime
> The Intrepid Traveler
> P.O. Box 531
> Branford, CT 06405

and we will refund the price of purchase.

> Chris and Kristal